NELSON

Nelson

by

C S Forester

CHATHAM PUBLISHING

LONDON

This edition published in Great Britain in 2001 by Chatham Publishing,
99 High Street, Rochester, Kent ME1 1LX

Distributed by Gerald Duckworth & Co. Ltd,
61 Frith Street, London W1D 3JL

First published in 1929

British Library Catloguing in Publication Data
A catalogue record for this book is available from the
British Library

ISBN 1 86176 178 3

Typeset by Dorwyn Ltd, Hants
Printed and bound by Cromwell Press Limited, Wilts

CONTENTS

I THE LETTERS AND DESPATCHES 1

II THE BEGINNING 12

III MODEST STILLNESS 34

IV THE MARRIAGE 45

V THE ENEMY 51

VI THE PATH OF GLORY 58

VII AGAMEMNON 71

VIII ST VINCENT AND SANTA CRUZ 89

IX THE NILE 102

X NAPLES 122

XI PALERMO 133

XII TWO MONTHS IN ENGLAND 150

XIII THE BALTIC 157

XIV THE CHANNEL AND MERTON 171

XV THE BLOCKADE 181

XVI THE PURSUIT 198

XVII TRAFALGAR 208

INDEX 227

List of Illustrations

Between pages 104 and 105

Letter dated 16 August (Taken from *The Dispatches and Letters of Lord Nelson*, Volume II)

Portrait of Nelson (The National Maritime Museum)

The Old Parsonage (Courtesy Michael Nash)

Frances Nelson (The Royal Naval Museum)

Emma as 'Nature' (Copyright the Frick Collection, New York)

Battle of the Nile (The National Maritime Museum)

Nile memorial (Courtesy Michael Nash)

Dido in Despair (The National Portrait Gallery, London)

Battle of Trafalgar (The National Maritime Museum)

The Death of Nelson (The National Maritime Museum)

Drawing of HMS *Victory* running up Channel (Tate Gallery)

HMS *Victory* (The Royal Naval Museum)

CHAPTER I

THE LETTERS AND DESPATCHES

H E has left behind him more than the memory and evidence of his achievements. There is also the large mass of his letters and despatches, gathered for the most part into a single series of volumes, with a large remainder to be found and read by those who can make the opportunity for themselves. In this respect as a subject of biography he resembles Napoleon, whose correspondence is readily available for examination, but in the most important other respect he is not comparable—in the sense of an object of study.

Contemporary studies of Nelson are woefully few. About Napoleon, for example, there can be no doubt as to his ability in the minor practice of his profession—innumerable witnesses can be called to show that he was as good a regimental officer as he was a general-in-chief; but in the case of Nelson very good evidence can be produced to show either that as a seaman he was excellent or only fair to middling. Good contemporary judges have said both the one and the other; and, confronted by such a direct position of opinion, the modern biographer seeks further written evidence, generally in vain. He is left to make what deductions are possible from the Letters.

1

Yet, although the Letters are the main source of information, they are a very satisfactory source. Study of them
calls up instant pictures of the writer, of his momentary state
of mind and of the permanent trend of his thoughts. His
anxieties, both public and private, his pleasures and his
hopes, can all be discerned. He becomes a much more
human, living, sympathetic being than ever Napoleon can,
perhaps because he was not given to intrigue or to the dis-
guising of his thoughts to those in his confidence. Even
Napoleon's love-letters, written before thirty, show us less of
Napoleon than Nelson's after forty show of Nelson. The
personal Nelson is always observable; that may be the reason
why he is so delightful a subject to read about or to write
about in comparison with, say, Wellington, whose brutally
impersonal correspondence is a mine of military information
but monotonous reading to the student of human nature.
This may, perhaps, stand as the excuse for the publication of
a biography of a seaman by a professional novelist whose
work consists in the study much more of human beings than
of maritime affairs; it seems a sound enough defence.

Very nearly everything we know of Shakespeare, to take
another example, is drawn and deduced from his work. The
minute amount of other evidence consists of meagre
scraps—his will, obscure references in parish records, doubtful tradition. It has become usual to conclude that we can
draw a mental picture of Shakespeare after an examination of
his work, which appears to be an exceedingly dangerous
assumption, the more dangerous, perhaps, because of the
impossibility of its contradiction. Yet no one can doubt that
we should know much more about Shakespeare if only he
had left some traces of his private life behind, in addition to
that allusion to his second-best bed. Nelson's *Hamlet* is the
Nile, his *Lear* is Trafalgar, his *Twelfth Night* is Copenhagen, his

Othello is his last Mediterranean campaign, his *Henry VIII* is St Vincent; but we have more than his works by which to know him.

We can read his own very acute estimate of his own professional worth, and his equally acute estimate of that of others, tinged, but not falsified, by his odd tendency to the hero-worship of those of his superiors in rank who are of proved merit, and of the youngsters of promise; tinged also by his petulant prejudice against the men of average talent with whom he has been at disagreement for some reason or other. We can read of his untiring patience and his extreme attention to details of organization—for that we need only draw attention to his elaborate arrangements for convoy during the last period of his Mediterranean command. We can read of his uneasiness under authority—uneasiness, not disloyalty—at the same time as we can study his open-handed delegation of authority to trustworthy subordinates and his right grip upon juniors with a tendency towards shiftiness. We can follow his own opinion of his health, which improves and declines in inverse ratio with the prospect of action. We can read his oddly flavoured letters to his wife, where 'esteem' usually takes the place of 'love', and where self-deceit leads him into tactless displays of a lack of feeling extraordinary in one so sensitive. We can study his progressive idealization of Lady Hamilton, idealization expressed in terms by high passion yet mingled with others of a jocose coarseness which leave one wondering. We can follow the gradual growth of his taste for applause and his simple delight in the admiration of others.

The Letters present a complex human problem to which one can turn again and again with increasing interest. Their style is consistent and attractively naïve. There is little trace of schooling (Nelson was only twelve when he left school) and the grammar is very frequently faulty—although in this case allowance must be made for the fact that many of the letters, clearly, were dictated, and hurriedly at that. Compared with Collingwood's or Cornwallis's despatches they are very inferior in this respect. They betray no sign of wide reading or of literary taste—the only quotation they contain which comes to mind is from *Henry V*, and that is misquoted—'But if it be a sin to covet glory'. Much more surprising is the fact that they contain hardly any hint of passion for his profession or for the sea. Nelson, who is so unreserved in his expression of his sentiment, never once baldly declares that he is glad to be a naval officer, and the reader cannot help harbouring the suspicion that his affection for the sea was never more than lukewarm, and even changed latterly into plain dislike; possibly because of his seasickness, or because of the difficulty, after the loss of his arm, of his boarding and quitting ships, and because the sea lay between him and the object of his beglamoured affection. The tenor of many of his later letters, indeed, is of his wish to retire and leave the sea, and settle down in some quiet corner of the country, or in Bronté for that matter, with his loved Emma—an experiment which it is probably just as well he never attempted to carry out.

Throughout the correspondence there runs a strongly religious sentiment, of whose sincerity we can have no doubt. As the son of one clergyman and brother of another, Nelson's early thoughts must have been given a religious turn, and he seems to have remained quite untouched by any of the fashionable fads of irreligion. When he declared that Almighty God had granted victory to His Majesty's fleet, he meant just what he said, for he often wrote much the same sort of thing to Lady Hamilton, which no one would expect him to do if he had the least shred of doubt. With all that, nevertheless, he never seemed to think there was anything sinful in his treatment of his wife or in his relations with Lady Hamilton—religious feeling and passionate desire between them worked their not unusual miracle of sanctifying the satisfaction of an intense longing, the intensity itself being the apparent grounds of the sanctification.

Along with this devout belief in God runs an equally devout belief in the institution of monarchy. Republicans are as damnable as atheists, and the more so as it seemed a usual occurrence for the former to be the latter as well. The man who did not believe in kings was the wrong kind of man and should not be allowed to exist; it is impossible to doubt that this is a very close approximation to Nelson's actual sentiment. The British system of government was the best the world could show, and, moreover, was so nearly perfect that to want to change it was a horrible crime. Even so shrewd a judge of men as Nelson had his judgment a little clouded when dealing with kings; his opinion of the King and Queen of Naples was a good deal higher than that held by the majority of students nowadays. The wretched Paul of Russia, even, rises in his eyes up to the standard of common humanity at least. His personal devotion to hard-working, conscientious, honest King George is more easy to understand.

It is only when the strongest of all human passions is at work that he is able to visualize Royalty without its aura, and then he writes about the Prince of Wales (George IV to be), whom he suspects of attempts to seduce Lady Hamilton, with an hysterical emphasis transcending even that employed about Frenchmen. For he had a most poisonous hatred of Frenchmen and all things French. It is not so hard to understand, seeing that for the last dozen years of his life Frenchmen were to be detested as Republicans and Atheists as well as the enemies of his country. His few months' stay

in France during his period of unemployment seems not at
all to have tempered this ungovernable aversion. Naturally
his ignorance of French literature and the fact that his
acquaintance with French people was restricted to members
of the official and military classes did not help to remedy this
state of affairs.

Indeed, there can be no denying that he was a man of very
limited range of interests, which makes the extent of his
knowledge of human nature all the more surprising. He had
little appreciation of art, although he extended a good-
humoured tolerance to Sir William Hamilton's twin passions
for collecting and for music—in one famous letter he lumps
together fiddlers, poets, whores and scoundrels in a single
scathing denunciation. Yet with all that he could form a very
clear estimate of public opinion, and he knew what would be
likely to catch the interest of the mass of human nature, as
witness not only the Trafalgar signal, but also the now hack-
neyed account of his career which he wrote for the *Naval
Chronicle*. That account bears the stamp of undoubted
journalistic talent; the manner in which unimportant but
interesting details are brought in to illustrate important
developments (his account of St Vincent gives another vivid
example) and the self-confident style are sound journalism.
It was only when his judgment was clouded by his unblessed
passion for Lady Hamilton that it became faulty in this
respect. He was unable to estimate the effect of his attach-
ment (and of his treatment of his wife) on public opinion,
and he was puzzled by the attitude assumed by the Court
towards Lady Hamilton—later in this book there will have to
be decided the debatable point as to whether this clouding
of his judgment did not extend to military and political
affairs as well.

In one respect at least the study of the Letters is not so

prolific in reward. That is in the effect Nelson had upon others. We catch glimpses of it, but we have to go to other authorities to appreciate fully his power of inspiring others, which was so largely responsible for his success. We can approach the matter indirectly; thus, study of his memoranda for battle leaves one quite doubtful as to whether orders of this sort would bring the stupendous results of Trafalgar or the Nile. The verbal explanations which ranked far higher in importance than the written memoranda counted for something too, but nobody can doubt that more important than either was the spirit of loyalty and emulation which he was successful in calling up—that threadbare declaration of Napoleon's, that in war it is not men that count but a man, is more applicable in the case of Nelson's campaigns than in any other example in modern military history. A fleet commanded by Nelson was equivalent to a fleet manned by Nelsons, and once that is said there is little room left for further labouring of the point.

For the bare wording of his orders gives a faint feeling of something missed; the Admirals and Captains who read those orders could supply that something out of their personal experience through actual contact with the magic personality, but we who live four generations later can only make good the deficiency with an effort. Not that the orders are equivocal or liable to misinterpretation (and we, of a later age, of personal experience of military orders ourselves, know how much that means), but they lack the literal clarity of Wellington's orders (perhaps Eton and the Military College, Angers, are responsible for that well-directed prose) and the exacting vigour of Napoleon's early orders. It is just possible that a fuller classical education or a modern course in essay-writing would have led to the casting of those orders in terms which would have clarified their significance to us.

But it is far more likely that their lack of instant appeal is a defect only due to his qualities of leadership.

Over one other matter discussed in the correspondence can the reader hesitate in doubt, and that is Nelson's proposals to employ a land force against the rear of a hostile army. It seems likely that it was fortunate that none of the Austrian or Piedmontese generals fell in with his suggestions during the Riviera campaign, and doubly fortunate that no English troops were at Nelson's disposition. Nelson seems to have formed a faulty estimate of what could and what could not be done with troops operating on land, and for any tangible result to have ensued from the plans he submitted enormous and unjustifiable risks would have had to be run. His plans match Napoleon's clever landsman's orders to the French fleet, and compare very unfavourably with Wellington's employment of the naval arm, for Wellington never asked sea power for more than sea power could reasonably be expected to perform. In this respect again Nelson's deficiency (if deficiency is admitted) must be attributed to his lack of general education in the wider sense.

Nowhere in the bulky volumes can there be found proof of a militaristic turn of mind. On occasions he thoroughly approves of the execution of mutineers and of strong measures to be taken against bad characters, but he never admires a fighting service just because it is a fighting service, nor has he a word to favour of war for war's sake. He is glad of peace when there is nothing to be gained by war, and although war brings him activity and employment, he finds in that no reason to rejoice at its coming. He will even hope for peace because he sees no object in the continuance of war, and not even the scoffer can advance the argument of a doubt as to his motives, because the sentiment occurs in a letter written before he made the acquaintance of Lady Hamilton.

His own ends, indeed, are the subject of few of the letters, and these are oddly contradictory. He could write flattering, even fulsome, letters of admiration to his superiors in the service, but no one reading them, even without knowledge of the circumstances in which they were written, could possibly think they were intended to curry favour for the writer. They display not so much indifference as a fatalist resignation regarding his future. Yet at the same time they show him to be most decidedly touchy regarding his present fame; if he has deserved praise he is annoyed when praise is not meted out to him, and he is annoyed, too, if the public acknowledgments of service in the way of titles of honour do not amount to what he has expected. But still, side by side with his complaints in this matter, go more fervent complaints still on behalf of his subordinates: good service to Nelson meant a loyal and untiring representation of that good service to headquarters.

He is rather pleased with his dukedom and peerage and diamond orders, although he is not above using the holding of honorary distinctions (by men he disliked) as the basis of a sneer—Captain Sydney Smith is 'the Swedish Knight', Admiral Orde is 'the Baronet'—just as Wellington's generals usually alluded to their awesome but unloved leader as 'the Peer'. He saw the ridiculous side of these distinctions at the same time as they flattered his childish vanity; perhaps the son of a poor parsonage could hardly help on occasions but feel there was something peculiarly special about titled gentry, and he was practical enough, too, to appreciate the spur the honours bestowed upon him might be to the others in the service.

One more constant impression received while reading the Letters is that of a vast potential energy awaiting employment. Even in the dark, unhappy period of his subordination to Keith in the Mediterranean, when his letters repeatedly bewail his ill health and his dissatisfaction with his situation, there is obviously behind the letters a possible source of energy only waiting to be tapped. Keith, poor man, honest, courteous, and even tactful though he was, was not the man to tap it, nor was Emma Hamilton the woman to direct it into its best channel. This was the worst time; during other periods no one can fail to be intensely impressed by the force and vigour of the personality behind the Letters, by the feeling that the writer would never, never leave undone the things that ought to be done, and, for that matter, would never cease from seeking to do things which it would occur to few as necessary to be done.

The general run of biography, in fact, tends to give the average reader a warped idea of humanity, because biography necessarily gives most of its attention to men who have done things. The biography of a very ordinary man might be tame reading, but it would be instructive when employed for purposes of comparison. Byng's despatches, for instance, written during the Minorcan campaign, show a man encountering difficulties at every turn, and simply without the force of character or the ingenuity to override them. In his own opinion Byng was innocent of everything charged expressly or by implication against him—undoubted facts had been too much for him, and to Byng that was both reason and excuse for his actions. A Byng cannot imagine a Nelson overcoming the difficulties, circumnavigating the facts, which have defeated him, for if he could he would cease to be a Byng and become a Nelson. To shoot a man because he has not by his own personal ability risen superior to circumstances may not be justice, as Voltaire pointed out, but at least it keeps his memory before the eye of the public as a standard of comparison with those men whose talents—

ingenuity, energy, imagination, experience, perseverance or anything else desirable—have enabled them to do so. In reading the chapters which follow it is necessary not merely to realize what Nelson did, but also what he might have left undone. That is the measure of greatness.

CHAPTER II

THE BEGINNING

THE meagre scraps of information—hearsay evidence, much of it—have been gathered together time and again; Southey made much of them in his mellifluous prose. They tell us almost nothing which is worth knowing. We cannot form a picture of the young Nelson with one half of the clarity of that of the young Napoleon, because the materials are wanting. There was no Bourrienne at Nelson's side to give us facts and descriptions (even erroneous ones) which might be used to fill the gap. The few anecdotes which we have could be told about almost any boy, and partly for that reason will not be told here. One noticeable fact is that the only motive which has been put forward for Nelson's desiring to go to sea is the wish to relieve his father of the burden of supporting him—hardly the most significant beginning of a career. We can trace no vocation such as Napoleon undoubtedly felt towards a military life.

However it was, this twelve-year-old son of a Norfolk parsonage took advantage of the fortunate possession of an uncle who was a Captain in the Royal Navy to be entered into the service at a time of expansion during an alarm of war. Captain Suckling was a man of some distinction in his profession, who later was to hold appointments of very considerable influence; at the moment it sufficed that, as Captain, he had a certain amount of patronage, being able to appoint on board his ship one or two children as 'captain's servants' and midshipmen. The alarm of war passed, and Captain Suckling was transferred to the *Triumph*, guardship in the Medway; his nephew nominally went with him. Yet while he was borne upon the books of the *Triumph* he was nevertheless sent to the West Indies as a seaman in a merchant vessel (he was not yet thirteen, remember) to learn as much of his trade as would be possible in the circumstances—more, apparently, than he would learn in a Medway guardship— and on his return he was employed in small boat work attendant upon the *Triumph*, which was the best method possible in the circumstances of habituating him to command and responsibility; the method is employed to this day in the navies of the world for the training of young officers. Constant work amid the shoals and currents of the Thames estuary did something more: it instilled that self-confidence amid this kind of peril which was to find its expression at moments of vital importance in English history at the Nile and at Copenhagen.

His next employment seems to have been obtained (unless Captain Suckling's influence had more to do with it than Nelson knew or admitted in his own biographical sketch) solely by that influence of his own personality, which was to become so powerful a means to advancement and success. An expedition into North Polar regions was being fitted out; the decision had been made that no boys were to accompany it, but Nelson, who was personally acquainted with Captain Lutwidge of the *Carcass* (a bomb-vessel which was one of the two ships to sail), succeeded in persuading him to include him among the exceptions. The expedition sailed, did nothing in particular, and came back again with not much knowledge gained; its one contribution to history is the well-worn anecdote which displays Nelson on the ice planning an attack on a polar bear with the butt end of his musket—an anecdote which is of no use to us, because, although it may illustrate extreme personal bravery, it hardly gives proof of the various other qualities which Nelson possessed.

Then on his return he found again how useful an uncle may be, for only a fortnight passed before he was employed again, this time on the corvette *Seahorse*, in which he sailed forthwith to East Indian waters. His period of pupation as a 'captain's servant' drew to an end at last on this voyage, and he became a full midshipman, presumably holding His Majesty's warrant, and on the way to exchanging it for His Majesty's commission. But after two years he was invalided home to England, a very sick man (or boy—he was just eighteen) with, implanted in him, apparently, the beginning of that weakness of constitution which was to go with him through life. All the same, there was a silver lining to the cloud, for eighteen months before his return his invaluable uncle had been appointed Comptroller of the Navy, and in consequence held a position of much patronage and more influence, the first proof of which to Nelson was his appointment as acting lieutenant on the *Worcester*, 64. Six months' service on the trade route to the Mediterranean followed, and then came his examination as lieutenant, which he passed well despite the fact that his uncle, who was on the board, concealed the relationship between them from his colleagues—proof enough, seemingly, that at this stage at least his seamanship was not so poor as to merit Codrington's description of him as 'no seaman'. Then Suckling did Nelson his last great service, by giving him his immediate appointment to *Lowestoft*, 32, about to sail to the Jamaica station, where fever and other incidentals of service were likely either to cut a career short or give it a decided impetus by rapid promotion.

And, moreover, there was likelihood of promotion. The discontent of the American colonies had, some time before, expanded into active revolt. British armies were moving ponderously about the rebel states, or being transferred hither and thither by sea; even sea power could not multiply the scanty British forces sufficiently to enable them to hold down the whole huge area which was in rebellion. Already American privateers had made their appearance, bearing letters of marque and reprisals, and their activity already foretold the time, close at hand, when the linen ships from Belfast to Liverpool would need convoy in the Irish Sea itself. Already French sympathy (or not so much sympathy with America as antagonism to England) had displayed itself in the shape of liberal treatment of privateers and the private despatch of succours. To pin down the privateers and to intercept the contraband called for a blockade of the whole American coast, and the vast number of ships necessary for that undertaking America was to learn to her cost when later she had to fight her own rebels. The demands of military convoy, of commerce protection, and of blockade meant an expanding navy, and an expanding navy meant at least that there would be no hindrance to promotion.

Sea power had come to the rescue of Quebec, and ensured Canada against invasion, had carried Howe from Boston to Halifax and back again to New York; it was sea power which would decide a protracted struggle one way or the other. A year before Nelson received his commission the Declaration of Independence made it certain that some at least of the rebels would fight it out to the bitter end, and Nelson had hardly crossed the Atlantic before Burgoyne started on his disastrous march to the Hudson. Lord George Germain neglected his duty, and the uninspired but painstaking efforts of King George III were nullified. Howe directed his own blow where it would do no harm; his victory on the Brandywine and his capture of Philadelphia could not save Gentleman Johnny Burgoyne from being hemmed in at Saratoga. The surrender of his six thousand British troops was a disaster worse than that of Kloster-Seven; to find its parallel in English history we must go back three and a half centuries to the relief of Orleans. The news resounded throughout Europe; it meant the redoubling of American effort, but, worse still, it meant the intervention of that European power whose influence was most to be dreaded. Now, if ever, were Lagos and Quiberon to be avenged.

The end of the Seven Years' War had found the French Navy in the condition usual to it at the end of a prolonged struggle with England. Fleet actions and attrition had worn down its material, and continued blockade had ruined its personnel. The French mercantile marine had been driven from the seas. Only a few bold privateersmen had continued the struggle, and by their efforts had given French maritime tradition a character which was for generations later to mould French naval policy. But, if French Ministers and French Admirals were to hold faulty theories about the employment of sea power, the genius of one French Minister was at least able to supply a French navy capable of action, even were that navy to be misdirected. Choiseul's tenure of power had been signalized by an extraordinary maritime development. The French Navy had been rebuilt. The loss of so many ships left room for the introduction of new designs, and, ship for ship, the French vessels which were built were superior to the English ones. The influence of the Court was brought into play to popularize the service among the indispensable nobility, with such good results that before long a Prince of the Blood Royal held a subordinate command in the fleet—which was more than Louis XIV himself effected, for in his reign a mere legitimatized prince only condescended to accept full command. To man the fleet a long service enlistment was instituted, and could be supplemented by an Inscription Maritime which would bring in a substantial though fleeting reinforcement. For the supply of officers the Naval College was revived—Colbert had begun it nearly a century before—so that cadets could receive professional training, to counterbalance the system by which budding English officers (Nelson among them, be it remembered) were trained in the extensive English merchant service. In a young navy a naval school implies a school of naval thought, and in a navy without past traditions of victory a school of naval thought will generally carry with it original thinking. Numerically the French fleet was little smaller than the British; its officers had largely received uniform training; it had developed ideas of its own—phrases which in 1914 were just as applicable to the Imperial German Navy. It was unfortunate, however (from the French point of view), that the ideas which were developed were not such as led to decisive success, with the result that a crisis which on the face of it was far more serious than any in 1914 was passed through without serious damage to England.

France had never in all her history enjoyed the relief from strain which is brought by a victory at sea. Her immediate independence, thanks largely, of course, to her powerful army, had never turned on the destruction of hostile ships. She could not look back to a vital victory similar to that of the English over the Armada. The reduction of her insurgent Huguenots had been achieved in the face of superior British sea power by reason of her overwhelming land power, of the misdirection of British effort, and of particular circumstances. Her victory at Beachy Head had been barren of

results through Louis XIV's infirmity of purpose.
Duquesne's splendid victories over Spaniards and Dutch in
the Mediterranean had brought small profit because little
had been at stake. On the other hand, La Gallissonnière's
partial action with Byng had won the magnificent prize of
Minorca, despite the fact that Byng was neither attacked nor
pursued with determination. The destruction of ships, to
the French naval mind, was ranked (was actually described,
in fact, by French writers) as merely the destruction of ships.
The consequent profits of such destruction seem, amazingly,
to have escaped detection, and French ingenuity was devoted
towards finding ends which sea power could attain while
avoiding decisive action and losses—a search which was only
not quite as barren of results as the contemporary endeavour
to find the philosopher's stone or to square the circle.

A tactical system, naturally, had to be developed to accord
with this perverted strategy. One was evolved and brought to
perfection, apparently more as the result of staff work than
by test in action, but which nevertheless succeeded in
baffling a whole generation of not too incapable British
Admirals. It consisted, as is well known, in taking the
leeward position in a fleet action, firing at the enemy's
spars in preference to his hulls, and, as soon as close action
was imminent, dropping away to leeward and repeating
the manoeuvre as often as was possible. Perhaps La
Gallissonnière was the man who devised the method, or perhaps it may have originated by accident during his action
with Byng off Minorca and been subsequently developed
after study by the leaders of naval thought. The whole principle of keeping the fleet out of harm's way, strategically if
possible and tactically if necessary, was sufficient, for most of
the period of the war just beginning, to disconcert the
English command, although it is strongly to be suspected

that the English did not realize until the closing period of the war that they were struggling against a particular system; especially when the entry of Spain and of the United Provinces into the war gave the allies a superiority of numbers which made, on occasions, the English Admirals just as chary of offering battle as their opponents were of accepting it. Yet when the situation began to dawn upon the English they began steadily to devise means to turn it to their advantage. Previously the long line ahead had brought good results when opposed to another line ahead which was equally willing to fight a battle; but it was a helpless formation, except under particular circumstances, when an attempt was to be made to compel battle. Something else had to be done; and, once the English had grasped that, pamphlets and private correspondence began to circulate in the endeavour to find a remedy.

According to some, Rodney found a remedy at the Saints, and some of those who believe this attribute the merit of his discovery to Rodney himself, some to his Flag-Captain, some to Clerk, whose pamphlet on fleet tactics has attracted more attention now than then, and some to plain, blind chance. What Rodney did was to take advantage of the windward position while engaging on opposite courses to break his opponent's line in two places (some say he did it by accident as a result of a flaw of wind and the blinding smoke), and though the battle ended in a victory and the capture of several prizes it was by no means as overwhelming a success as such a manoeuvre would seem to make likely. This again has been attributed to Rodney's lack of energy, to bad blood between him and his juniors, and to misfortune. Incidentally, it may also be mentioned that both at the time and since it has been denied that Rodney's manoeuvre contributed towards the victory. Cornwallis, who later was to prove himself a bold, persevering and thoughtful sailor, was hot against his Admiral's conduct; there was quite a large body of opinion that maintained that the victory would have been greater if the action had been maintained in single line ahead—and that point, again, is clouded by the fact that in this particular case the French were fighting under conditions when even to them an action seemed likely to be less damaging than refusal of action.

Even as late in the war as this, a fleet in action was nominally subject to the fighting instructions drawn up a century earlier by James II when Lord High Admiral, which laid down the line ahead as the formation for battle and strictly forbade any captain to leave the line. It was these instructions which had formed the basis of the charges against Mathews after Toulon, and which had preyed so much upon the mind of the wretched Byng at Minorca. There can be no denying that a large conservative opinion still held to the spirit of these instructions and vigorously opposed the suggested innovations of the new school, despite the lessons of Keppel's unfortunate action off Ushant, of Arbuthnot's indecisive battles and of various other incidents during a prolonged war.

So that during Nelson's early, most impressionable years (he was always ready to receive new impressions all his life) his attention was constantly being drawn to this, the ultimate problem of every naval officer: how best to bring a number of ships into action with a hostile fleet without crippling damage, and, following on that problem, the equally difficult one of how to arrange to have a greater number of guns bearing than the enemy. The problems are easy to state, but well-nigh impossible to solve, given an enemy of fair skill and of some reluctance to enter into action; the solution is as hard to perceive at the present day as it was a hundred and fifty years ago. Neither Jutland nor August 10th, 1904, displayed the ability of a superior fleet to close with an absconding enemy, which is why Nelson's suggestions on the matter are of such peculiar interest; furthermore, it is worth noticing that Nelson's ideas of tactics while he was still a very young captain were considered sufficiently sound and illuminating for him to be indicated to Prince William as the man to go to for instructions.

Nor was it only to tactics that Nelson's attention was drawn. The American War of Independence is, from the naval point of view, one long series of missed opportunities—more so, that is to say, even than the general run of wars. Both the English and the allies threw away chances. There was the chance of crushing a fragment of the French Fleet at Newport, RI, with less risk of failure (Mahan endorses the declaration) than there was at Copenhagen. There were the half-dozen opportunities thrown away by the French in the West Indies, leaving out of account those which were rendered unsuitable by Hood's vigour and resolution. There were the chances which came Rodney's way before the battle of the Saints, and, above all and more important than any, there were the whole months of opportunity enjoyed by the Allied Fleets when they swept the Channel in superior numbers and the British fleet was constrained to avoid them—the only time that a Continental fleet has commanded the narrow seas since Beachy Head, and as lacking in results. To Nelson, who, by a series of chances, lived on the fringe of history, as it were, during all this period, the realization of what was being missed was intense and impressive. It is to these years that his later resolves of never to lose an hour or waste a wind can be traced: and what those resolves meant to England it is the purpose of this book to show.

We left him newly arrived in Jamaica in July, 1777, a lieutenant not yet nineteen. Then we find him gaining the
interest and the affection of Captain Locker of the *Lowestoft*,
so much so that when the deadliness of climate sent Locker
home on sick leave his earnest recommendation decided
Nelson's transfer, in July 1778, as third lieutenant of the
Bristol, in which Sir Peter Parker, Admiral commanding the
station, flew his flag. Once more Nelson's personality made
itself felt. Both Parker and his wife grew fond of him (and,
reading between the lines of various letters, it seems safe
enough to conclude that it was desirable to stand well with
Lady Parker if one wished to stand well with Sir Peter), and
after death or promotion had removed two of Nelson's
immediate superiors in three months Parker gave Nelson his
next important step by promoting him Commander in the
Badger brig, December, 1778. Captain Suckling, that fairy
uncle, had died the very same month as Nelson went to the
Bristol, and Nelson was now without any influence other
than what he could procure for himself. It is this fact which
makes his rapid promotion so impressive; it was either his
talents or his apparent promise of talent which affected
Parker, if it was not a rapidly developed personal affection.
Nelson, in fact, when he lost his uncle, found in Parker an
ally who in the circumstances would be of more immediate
use to him even than a Comptroller of the Navy. And it does
not seem to be over-straining probability when we decide
that personal affection was not Parker's sole or principal
motive, because his possession of an eye for talent is confirmed by his simultaneous promotions of Collingwood, who
succeeded Nelson in a number of different appointments.

In June, 1779, thanks to Admiral Parker, Nelson attained
Captain's rank in His Majesty's Navy, at the mature age of
twenty. He had been Commander for just six months; and

despite the fact that for some years past a desperate war had
been waged in every sea in the world he had yet to see a shot
fired in anger. Promotion at this rate is inconceivable to our
minds nowadays, and throws a lurid light on the power and
responsibility of Admirals in command of stations in those
days of difficult communication and much delegation of
authority. Yet Nelson's rise was not phenomenal; it was dis-
tinctly more rapid than that of the majority, but it was
equalled and surpassed by a number of his contemporaries,
which constitutes a fair argument against Lord Fisher's later
factious dictum in favour of favouritism. The system which
produced Nelson produced also uncounted swarms of other
Admirals who were found wanting and who languished
undistinguished as Port Admirals or without employment. It
can at least be considered equally as risky and wasteful as the
modern arrangement which calls for seniority as well as
selection, and it undoubtedly was more liable to abuse;
although comparison is difficult, because of the undeniable
fact that in those days a naval officer had less to learn in the
technique of his profession than he would have nowadays—
and this in despite of the opposing fact that the more distinguished of the flag officers of the last war were men who
previously had received promotion out of their turn (for service on land, in large part), and had thereby escaped some of
the years of preliminary training which the modern system
accepts as necessary to the best practice of the naval art.

As a Captain, Nelson was no longer in need of friends to
procure him promotion, which would come to him automat-
ically; what he was in need of was employment, and with a
war in progress and the navy expanding there was no fear of
his being in want of that for same time to come. He had been
posted to the *Hinchinbrook*, one of the smaller frigates of the
squadron. A momentary scare of a French attack upon

Jamaica (d'Estaing at the moment was sweeping through the West Indies with a gigantic armada) gave him promise of active service, and as soon as the danger passed he was transferred again from his command of the batteries of Fort Charles (at Port Royal) and went forth on ordinary cruiser duty, making a number of captures—Spain had just entered the war and Spanish ships were good prize—which were much to his profit under the old system of prize money, by which the Captain of a fortunate cruiser could accumulate an enormous fortune. This early financial benefit, nevertheless, was not a true augury, because Nelson (largely because of his insistence on being employed in fighting rather than in commerce destruction) later made very little money, comparatively, out of these profitable sidelines.

Even at this period of his career fighting came to him as a matter of course. There was a certain Dalling, Governor of Jamaica, who found himself, now that d'Estaing had passed on to Savannah, free from the imminent menace of attack and with the troops and stores accumulated for that contingency at his disposal. With a temerity which remains astonishing (but which may have been of that class which made the British Empire what it is) Dalling proceeded to divest himself of the services of five hundred of his scanty regular troops and to launch a wild expedition upon the South American mainland. There is an oddly familiar ring about most of the details of this campaign. On the map it looked as if success would bring gigantic benefits. From Atlantic to Pacific the line across Nicaragua by way of San Juan river and Lake Nicaragua has repeatedly appeared to thoughtful men as the most advantageous route for commerce, and the Spaniards actually employed it as such, but only to a small extent, because the Panama route, expensively maintained, was, slightly, both more practicable and more convenient.

But on the map, and after only casual study, the object of the expedition seemed both easy of attainment and most eminently desirable. There was a fort or two to be taken, and a hundred miles of river to be ascended, before command of Lake Nicaragua could be attained, but that command (apparently, though, authority did not really consider what was to happen after that) once attained, surely the trade routes could be controlled, an expedition pushed on to the Pacific, a naval force created there, and booty comparable with that of Drake or Anson captured! There would be quantities of prize money. Dalling despatched to carry out this promising scheme a force of five hundred infantry and one small ship of war. Whether or not England, pressed to extremity elsewhere, would be able to exploit any successes they might achieve (successes not to be expected by a sane judgment) was more than he was capable of knowing. Moreover, he sent the expedition at the wrong time, and after profitless discussion. If only he had committed one more mistake, and sent the naval force first and the troops later, the analogy would be complete between this effort and a much more costly one of some time later which was also inspired by a cursory study of the map and a gross misestimate of probabilities and resources.

Nelson himself, writing twenty years later, thoroughly condemned the time of despatch of the expedition and the corresponding arrangements, although he did not display such acute disapproval of the whole wild squandering of effort, but Nelson, as we know, held (to say the least of it) lofty ideas as to the effectiveness of small bodies of troops landed from ships. He brought to the business all the splendid energy and determination he gave to all enterprises in which he was engaged. His orders only were to convoy the troops to the harbour of San Juan de Norte (Greytown), but

on his arrival inspection of possibilities on the spot convinced him that it would be as well to continue to give the
army his assistance. The force had arrived three months too
late, for the water in the river had by this time (April) fallen
too low to allow of easy navigation. Mosquito Indians (whom
some describe as the finest canoe-men in the world) were
recruited from the neighbouring coast, and with these and
fifty seamen and marines Nelson proceeded to conduct five
hundred troops, with baggage and stores, including siege
equipment, upstream along a tropical river encumbered with
sandbars. He succeeded, forcing his way through to the fort
of San Juan, an outpost of which he stormed on his arrival.
But the fort itself was a tougher nut to crack. The officer
commanding the land forces refused to attempt to storm
(and seeing what his position was, in a hostile country with
communications running back down the torrent he had
ascended with so much difficulty, one can hardly blame him)
and decided to proceed by regular approaches. Nelson took
charge of the guns in the batteries while the parallels were
being made, and at length the fort succumbed to the
inevitable but lengthy attack of siege operations. But Nelson
was not present to witness this success, for he had been
recalled to take command of a much larger frigate, the *Janus*.
His health was ruined for the time, nevertheless. Exposure,
malaria, yellow fever—all the plagues which came to be so
well known when first the French and then the Americans
were labouring at Panama a few miles to the south—were let
loose upon the wretched English. Fort San Juan fell, indeed,
and a hardy handful of soldiers struggled through to Lake
Nicaragua, but the splendid dreams of Governor Dalling
proved only to be dreams. The exhausted survivors could
effect nothing, and the expedition was withdrawn, after
three-quarters of its numbers had perished. It was a result

similar to that attendant upon at least a dozen similar efforts by England during the two centuries following the Stuart accession.

Nelson himself was a very sick man on his return to Jamaica. His command of the *Janus* came to a speedy end, and he was sent home to England at his own request as an invalid on board the *Lion*, Captain Cornwallis. Cornwallis, one of the most promising of the Captains in the navy, was later to sustain the burden of the blockade of Brest while Nelson commanded in the Mediterranean; a hard-fighting officer, it was his fate never to command in a successful fleet action, but to have his reputation largely based on a skilful retirement in face of superior numbers. It was from his lips during this voyage that Nelson must have received personal information about what had been taking place in the other theatres of war, where time and again fleet had encountered fleet with small result. For five months in England Nelson was a nearly helpless invalid. He himself attributed his weakness largely to gout—'gout in the breast'—but prolonged service in the West Indies, in districts reeking with malaria and yellow fever, explains his illness much more satisfactorily.

After his cure at Bath he was appointed to the small frigate *Albemarle*, which ship he himself commissioned. His letters to his brother and to Captain Locker (late of the *Lowestoft*, a man to whom history is greatly in debt in consequence of his preservation of the numerous letters written him by Nelson) are full of his ideas about the ship, her officers and her crew. He has nothing but praise for them, as was always to be the case with anything under his command. Perhaps it was Nelson's willingness to be pleased (not a decided characteristic of the Naval officer of that or any other age) which led some of his contemporaries to describe him as 'no seaman', but perhaps at the same time it was the root of his popularity and the devotion he always inspired. However it may be, it is worth comparing Nelson's 'I am perfectly satisfied with both officers and ship's company' and 'Not an officer or man in her I would wish changed' with Wellington's description of the army that bore unflinching such terrible punishment at Waterloo as 'a despicable army', every man of which 'had enlisted for drink', and with the same general's insulting general order in the autumn of 1812 to the army which had just won the battle of Salamanca; and there can be no doubt either of the love borne towards Nelson or of the dislike (respectful dislike) evinced for Wellington. The clearest proof of the greatness of the two men is the way in which they allowed for these factors, the one when he plunged into action at the Nile, sure of the most earnest co-operation of his subordinates, and the other in half a hundred Peninsular actions where he made sure of implicit obedience by being always on the spot where a decision was to be reached.

But this new command with which Nelson was so pleased bade fair to be the death of him, for he was despatched to bring home a convoy from the Baltic in December, after three years in the tropics and a crippling illness. He remarked pithily in a letter on his return, 'I have been almost frozen on the other side of the water'. As it might be to make amends, the Admiralty's next decision was to send him to the East Indies, where Suffren and Hughes were fighting out their long-drawn struggle. But chance dictated that history should be deprived of the example of Nelson engaged as a subordinate in a fleet action fought out with determination; a storeship drove from her anchors on board the *Albemarle* and did her so much damage that she had to go into dock at Portsmouth and was not fit for service for three months. As a result Bickerton sailed without him, and the *Albemarle* was sent with the *Dædalus* on convoy duty to Quebec, where, despite Nelson's earlier fears, the climate appears to have restored him to the best of health. The chance that threw the store-ship upon the *Albemarle* did more than keep Nelson from service in Indian waters: it brought him into contact with one of the greatest of English Admirals (perhaps the greatest of the period), Hood. Nelson's professional achievements so far were very small compared with those of many of his fellow captains. A commerce-destroying voyage from the St Lawrence had been successful (although pecuniarily unprofitable to Nelson because the captures failed to reach port), and he had succeeded in throwing off the pursuit of four French ships of the line and a frigate, who discovered him upon the clearing of a fog, by running in amongst the shoals beside Boston Bay: the ships of the line broke off the pursuit, and were imitated by the frigate as soon as Nelson hove to and challenged action. But these services, and the taking of Port Juan, were all Nelson had to his credit when duty brought him into New York, where lay Hood and the main fleet. The battle of the Saints had been fought and won the previous spring; Hood had left the Caribbean Sea in pursuit of the French, and was now about to return to the West Indies. There was likelihood of vigorous action, and Nelson's whole heart was set upon sharing in it.

That he attained his wish is a further proof of the power of his personality. There is little enough to be surprised at, presumably, in Hood's agreeing to take the *Albemarle* with the fleet: the remarkable thing is that Admiral Digby, Nelson's immediate superior, should have consented to part with her, when the blockade duties upon which he was engaged called for the employment of as many units as he could gather into his command. Nelson, however, had already approached him on the matter, and had thrust aside

Digby's unbelieving remonstrance that his present station was the best for prize money, and had displayed so much sincerity that when Hood approached Digby on the subject the latter yielded. Nelson had once more placed himself in a situation to obtain the favour which might mean so much to him, and he obtained that favour, as he always did. Hood's notice of him now brought him later the *Agamemnon* and all the opportunities of the Mediterranean service.

Even at the moment he became a man of mark. Hood, whose conduct in half a dozen actions showed him to be a man who knew his subject, came speedily to the opinion that Nelson was an original and sound thinker on tactics, and to this he drew the attention of Prince William, soon to be Duke of Clarence, and later Lord High Admiral and eventually William IV. Moreover, Nelson's extraordinary disinterestedness in wishing to leave the profitable cruising ground off the New England coast attracted sufficient attention for the *Albemarle* to be ordered to sail for the West Indies two days after the main fleet, so that any prize she took would not have to be shared—a favour which, as ever, brought in nevertheless small profit to Nelson, although after she had rejoined she captured a ship full of stores intended for the French fleet. They proved, in the end, to be stores which enabled the English fleet to go to sea much less ill-equipped than would otherwise have been the case.

But no decisive results attended the campaign. Vaudreuil devoted most of his energy to keeping out of Hood's way, and Hood was unable to get within reach of him. His frigates (Nelson's among them) sought him in vain. One proof of French activity was encountered by Nelson, when he found that Turk's Island, one of England's oldest colonies, had fallen to a small force of French troops and a squadron. Nelson made a prompt effort to recover the place, taking

under his orders such English ships as he could whose captains were junior to him, but the island was prepared for
resistance and the attempt failed. His landing force was too
small to be pitted against the French infantry, and there were
batteries ready to oppose any attack by sea upon the town.
Nelson called off his men and the incident closed.

And two years before an apprehensive note in one of
Nelson's letters had sounded the beginning of the end of the
war. 'I much fear for Lord Cornwallis; if something was not
immediately done, America is quite lost.' The letter had
dealt with Graves's report on his action against Grasse in the
Chesapeake. 'Something' was not immediately done—there
was little left that could be done by that time, and
Cornwallis, hemmed in at Yorktown and with Grasse
between him and the sea-borne succour, had surrendered.
With his capture had passed England's last chance of the
reconquest of the revolted colonies. Sea power badly
employed, and helped in the last resource by good luck, had
freed America, although that same power skilfully handled
might have dealt a blow at England herself from which she
could not have recovered. The allied naval and military
strength had devoted itself to wasteful and generally unsuccessful attempts upon unessential objectives. America was
free, which was a deceptively brilliant proof of victory. West
Indian islands had changed hands. Minorca had fallen,
although Gibraltar still held out, thanks to amazing bad management on the part of the French and Spaniards and brilliant service by the English. The allies had spent their
energy on clumsy hacking at the limbs instead of striking
with all their strength at the heart. They had allowed themselves to be imposed upon by the phantom of the 'fleet in
being' which had deterred the French once before at a vital
moment in William III's reign. Their navies, even as before,

had decayed and wilted under the stress of war, which had at
the same time strengthened and developed the British military marine. Warfare for the moment had lost its sting; its
stakes had become national prestige rather than national
existence. A plan of campaign which threatened the life of a
nation had become unthinkable on account of its very scope.
The pedantry and cynicism of the eighteenth century, its
objectless irreligion, had combined with the developed eti-
quette of international relations and hostilities to set warfare
upon much the same footing as Olympic games in the public estimation. Only when the French Revolution came to
make the existence of a government dependent upon military victory did war regain its overwhelming importance in
the scheme of things. It is one of the ironies of history that
the wealthiest nation in the world should owe its birth to a
war which had aimed so low.

The French Government was tottering towards bank-
ruptcy. No great personality had arisen in France who could
direct French effort or coerce France's allies. England was
humiliated and ready to admit the loss of her American possessions, and France could hardly visualize a greater success,
flinched from paying the price such success would demand,
and had come to doubt its attainment. England, on the other
hand, was resigned to the loss of America, and she was
healed in her self-esteem by Rodney's victory at the Saints
and by the negative success of the defence of Gibraltar. In
such an international state of mind peace was made.

Hood and his fleet were ordered home, and Nelson followed him, after first accompanying Prince William to
Havana. That gave him contact again with Royalty, which
was always desirable in a service wherein employment was
largely a matter of patronage, and on his arrival in England
Hood took him to Court, presented him to the King, and,

apparently, sang his praises to Lord Howe and the other people who mattered. One can hardly decide which is the more surprising, Hood's discernment in perceiving the promise of this junior Captain, whose war service only included the disastrous Nicaraguan campaign and the abortive attempt on Turk's Island, or the power of the personality of this young man of twenty-four in impressing itself upon the notice of the hard-bitten Admiral, who was surrounded by captains twice as old with records twenty times as distinguished.

CHAPTER III

MODEST STILLNESS

WITH the end of the war English society swarmed into France, just as it did after the Peace of Amiens and after Waterloo. With it went Nelson from a mixture of motives. One was the desire to learn French; another was the desire to live cheaply, for Nelson was in his usual condition of having slightly less money than he believed he needed, which condition may be attributed partly to unqualified carelessness and partly to careless generosity. He had left England with the determination not to seek employment during peace-time, and with the expectation of spending at least six months in France; he came back to England in two months and immediately set about trying to obtain a ship. His letters afford no distinct statement of the motive of this complete reversal of his plans. He found himself entirely out of sympathy with the French nation despite a flirtation or two (wordless ones) with pretty girls with whom he had hardly a word in common. He disliked French manners, habits and points of view. But, besides all this, he fell in love with an English clergyman's daughter at St Omer, wrote to an uncle for an allowance in the event of marriage, almost certainly received the promise of one, and did not marry. Presumably the girl refused him, after a courtship which cannot have endured more than two months; but seeing that his

letter to his uncle is dated after his arrival in England, it is
just as probable that he never made a proposal, but thought
better of the idea and went to sea, either to put himself out
of the way of making it or else because the desire for employment suddenly overcame all other motives. However it was,
Nelson came to London, called on Lord Howe, dined with
him, and discarded all the wild plans he had hinted at to his
Uncle Suckling—plans for applying for command of the East
India Company's marine, for seeking a government sinecure,
for applying for a guard-ship—and accepted the First Lord's
offer of a frigate. Having thus set himself again to the dili-
gent practice of his profession, the change of ministry which
occurred simultaneously (January, 1784) did not disappoint
him. He was given command of the *Boreas*, in which he sailed
from Woolwich in April, 1784.

He had hoped for the East Indies, but the Admiralty
decreed that it was to the West Indies that the *Boreas* should
be despatched. We might say that this was one of the occasions which we can pick out as definitely affecting subsequent history, but we cannot be sure. We know what Nelson
did on the West Indian station, but we cannot even guess to
what activities his restless energy and his quest for responsibility would have led him in the East Indies. The Admiral
commanding on the Leeward Islands station was Sir Richard
Hughes, a man of undistinguished record. He was a man of
only modest ability, and not one of ingenuity nor of vast
energy. He was not successful in getting the best out of captains and his crews, and was a steady, easy-going, not-too-
intelligent gentleman. His wife, who, with his children,
sailed for the West Indies in the *Boreas*, was of different
stuff, and it is to her that we owe several sympathetic and
intelligent letters about Nelson at this period. Nelson clearly
won her affection at the start (in a letter to his brother, who

came with them as chaplain, he describes her as a 'fine talkative lady,' and was to benefit from the fact, just as once he had benefited from the affection of Lady Parker.

The commissioning of the *Boreas* gave Nelson the usual bits of patronage associated with Captain's rank; it was his turn to select 'captain's servants' as budding admirals, and he was able to take the Reverend W Nelson, his elder brother, as chaplain. This brother had long hankered after such an appointment, despite Nelson's arguments that he would find it very unpleasant under a tactless captain. Even under Horatio the one experience seems to have been sufficient, and he never tried the experiment again. The boys and midshipmen, on the other hand, were treated with the sympathy one would expect. Southey's brilliant paraphrases of Lady Hughes's letters have told us all about how he would coax timid youngsters into making the ascent to the masthead, and how he took the noon observation along with them daily—an odd little example, this, of the golden disciplinary rule of never giving an order one is not ready to carry out oneself—and how, on his arrival at Barbados, he laid down his rule of always being accompanied by one of the boys when dining with Governors and similar gentlemen, in order to habituate them to polite society.

This commission, all the same, was not going to be a peaceful one without incident. Even before the *Boreas* left English waters things began to happen: first the pilot ran her aground, then Nelson had to intervene in a quarrel between a Dutch captain and his English crew, who apparently wanted to leave the Dutch service and were unable to because they were not allowed to take their belongings with them. Nelson settled the business by the high-handed method of ordering the Dutchman not to be allowed to leave his moorings nor to have any communication with the shore until men and goods were set free. What the Dutchman thought about it can well be guessed, but apparently Nelson's action was approved by his superiors—a King's ship in the Narrow Seas had an overwhelming authority. Next, at Portsmouth, Nelson, while riding round the town, was run away with by his horse, and after being carried all round and through the town, only escaped a worse accident by throwing himself off at full speed at the cost of some nasty bruises, while his companion (Nelson only says 'a young girl' and we are left in the dark as to who she was) was only saved by some brave unknown catching her horse's bridle.

A voyage begun under these auspices could hardly help being crammed with incident even without Nelson in command; as it was, Nelson made the most of the opportunities which came his way. Quite early in the cruise a restless note creeps into his letters. One of his fellow frigate captains is 'no more of an officer as a captain than he was as a lieutenant'. Admiral Hughes is 'tolerable, but I do not like him ... his wife has an eternal clack'. In short, 'I detest this country ... the Admiral and all about him are great ninnies'. The only man worth counting on is Collingwood, with whom he was in infrequent contact.

It was not long before this fretting, restless young man of twenty-six found ample trouble to occupy his mind; he succeeded in a couple of months (as soon as the hurricane season was over, in fact, and activity was possible) in stirring up a couple of hornets' nests. The first brought him much more trouble than the second, in this fashion. The Navigation Acts laid down that trade with British colonies could only take place in British-built ships manned to the extent of at least three-quarters by British subjects. The Leeward Islands possessed an extensive trade with the United States of America, which was carried on by American-built ships manned by

American subjects. Up to two years before, until England recognized America's independence, this had been legal enough, but things were different now. Hughes, easy-going man, wished to let well alone. He had no orders from home on the subject, and his mild good sense may have protested against the idea of arbitrarily interfering with a business which was contributing its mite towards the wealth of the world. Nelson, carrying Collingwood with him, saw matters in a different light. He claimed that the Statutes of the Admiralty specifically ordered all captains to enforce the Navigation Acts. That was the argument he employed, although from the tenor of his letters one is led to suspect that other leading motives were his restlessness and his desire to show the Americans what they had lost by their treason and revolt. Collingwood, on the other hand, brought into action the conservative argument that the Navigation Acts were helpful to the growth of England's mercantile marine and augmented her prestige. Between them they pinned down Hughes into an admission that they ought to see the Act carried into execution, and with that off went Nelson to St Kitts, where, to the consternation of islanders and Americans alike, the *Boreas* fell into the placid life of colonial export like the stork among the frogs, turned American shipping away, and generally caused trouble.

Nevertheless, no sooner was Nelson's influence removed from Hughes than the latter was beset by arguments from all in the islands pointing out the disturbance likely to be caused and the doubtful legality of his orders. Hughes, as was only to be expected of one of his temperament, tried to shuffle off responsibility by sending orders to his captains to be guided by the wishes of the governors of individual islands, and not to interfere with trade if the governors did not desire them to do so. And, naturally, the governors, whose main idea was to keep their people contented and prosperous, did not want the Acts enforced. General Shirley, Governor of St Kitts, promptly told Nelson so and requested him to leave off his present course of action. No effort of imagination is needed to realize what Nelson thought of this business of being put under a soldier's orders and required to break an Act of Parliament of which he highly approved. Shirley was sent away with a flea in his ear (Nelson writes that he 'trimmed him up'), for nothing Hughes could do could make Shirley Nelson's hierarchical superior. As to Hughes himself, Nelson came to the most serious decision an officer of a fighting service could possibly take. He wrote to him announcing that he declined to obey his orders in this matter, and he gave public notice that he would continue to enforce the Navigation Acts as heretofore. Hughes dilly-dallied; the poor man had been thrust into a position of unexpected unpleasantness, and he had not the force of will to carry through his intentions. Nelson's defiance called forth at first the natural response, to supersede him and court-martial him for disobedience, but Hughes found his other captains hesitant about the legality of his decision regarding the permission to trade, which made him rather doubtful as to what would be the verdict of the court-martial, and at the same time gave him to fear lest he should receive similar defiance from any other captain sent to St Kitts. A stronger man might still have carried the matter through with a high hand—we can picture Jervis or Hood in such a situation—but Hughes hesitated. He allowed Nelson to proceed, and assumed the extraordinary attitude of a dis-interested observer. During some of the trouble which Nelson's activity brought down on the head of his captain, Hughes was actually present with his flag flying in the port, and yet he made no attempt to interfere. Neither Americans nor islanders were going to give up a profitable trade without a struggle; when Nelson displayed his determination by sending into port for condemnation an American vessel which was caught in the act, they attempted to obtain British registration for their ships, only to find that Nelson refused to be influenced by such registration, and continued to send the ships in. Not even a legal decision in Nelson's favour, confirming every one of his actions, ended the struggle. The inhabitants of Nevis incited the masters of the American vessels to bring suit against Nelson for assault and imprisonment. Four thousand pounds damages were claimed, and for weeks Nelson had to remain on board the *Boreas* to avoid arrest. But news of the business at last reached England, along with a memorial from Nelson to the King stating his position. Back came despatches; Hughes was highly commended for his zeal in suppressing the trade, and instructions were given for the defence of Nelson at the Government's expense and with the approval of the local governors.

Nelson was nominally cleared of all possibility of blame. Had his first judgment been at fault, he would have been liable not merely to dismissal from the navy for his disobedience, but also for damages for his disturbance of trade, to an amount which the exasperation of the trade would have raised to a figure sufficient to leave him for life in a debtor's prison. That was the stake he had risked; his reward was nothing except the knowledge of having done his duty. He received no official statement of approval of his actions. His further employment in peace-time was rendered unlikely. He had antagonized powerful interests outside the service, and within it he had infuriated Hughes and gained himself a reputation as a restless customer, the sort of captain no Admiral who valued his peace of mind (and most Admirals do) would willingly see under his command—as long as peace endured.

His motive cannot instantly be stated. First and foremost, of course, was the desire to do his duty; that goes quite without saying. But there were other factors: his restless energy, his poor opinion of Hughes, his antagonism towards the Americans—all played their part. And, obscurely but certainly, there was a slight additional motive. Nelson's independence of mind was such that a course of action which he thought right was more attractive still if acted upon without orders, and much more attractive if acted upon against orders. Let it be repeated that Nelson had to be sure that the course of action was right before he entered upon it against orders. But, once he was sure, that course of action attained additional attractiveness if to act upon it meant disobeying some one of whom he did not hold too high an opinion. The same trait is not unusual in the character of most people, but generally it avoids notice in consequence of being overlain by fear of responsibility or dislike of attracting attention. Nelson offered more than one example of it later in his career.

This subject of controversy was not the only one which arose during that eventful commission. At the time when the Navigation Acts affair was at its height Nelson in the *Boreas* came to Antigua, and there found a broad pendant flying by the authority of the Commissioner of the Navy, who happened to be a Captain Moutray, much Nelson's senior, but in civil employ and not military. Nelson, as senior captain in employment, promptly announced that the pendant had no business to be flying; and, when he was informed that Hughes had issued orders to his captains to conform to any directions of Moutray's, he denied that Hughes had any power to give such orders, and it was only to save causing Moutray unnecessary pain that he refrained from ordering the pendant to be struck at once. Once more Hughes submitted to the energetic vigour of this subordinate (Hughes was, of course, quite wrong in trying to put his captains under command of a half-pay officer) and the Admiralty bore Nelson out—in this case, however, with the sharp comment that it might have been better if Nelson had consulted first with Hughes before taking control himself. A very sound opinion; but the Admiralty did not know Hughes as well as Nelson did. This very comment goes to illustrate the attraction the disobeying of ill-conceived orders had for Nelson.

This business occurred during the months of the hurricane season, during which Nelson was in close contact with Moutray. Curiously, he seems to have made a friend of Moutray despite the disagreement, and, perhaps not so curiously, he made a much greater friend of his wife. To Mrs Moutray he gave all his devotion for a time, and her departure with her husband left him, so he wrote, without a single valuable friend in the islands. They were rather charming letters he wrote to Mrs Moutray and about her; the lack of literary grace is more than made up by his wistful sincerity. 'I am really an April day; happy on her account, but truly grieved were I only to consider myself.' He wrote to his brother to see that his sister met Mrs Moutray that winter at Bath. 'What an acquisition to any female to be acquainted with', he writes.

Then came Prince William Henry to the station, to serve as captain under Nelson's command. The two got on well together, and Nelson held a high opinion of the Prince's professional talents—though how much of it was due to Nelson's inherent respect for Royalty cannot be said. There is a portentous supplement in the letter stating this opinion—'Some others, I have heard, will tell another story'. Anyway, Prince William found himself involved in a disagreement with one of his lieutenants, who demanded a court-martial and raised endless trouble by that demand, which eventually resulted in the despatch by Nelson of two vessels to Jamaica. The Admiralty's reply to the report sent in by Nelson bore the ominous rider— 'My lords are not satisfied with the reasons you have given. . . . You will be answerable for the consequence, if the Crown should be put to any expense upon that account'. So much for Royalty.

The last occurrence of note on the station was the declaration to Nelson by a merchant of Antigua (after a fruitless approach to Prince William) concerning frauds upon the Admiralty alleged to have been committed during the last war at various West Indian dockyards. Nelson took the matter up, but (as must necessarily be the case when a number of powerful people are interested in the suppression of evidence) it took years to sift the truth of the matter. Nelson was bothered both by this and by a renewal of the Nevis prosecution long afterwards, while he was on half-pay in England. There can be small wonder that he wrote, as he did, 'This last year I have been plagued to death', although there is the very pertinent reply to this complaint that nearly all his troubles he brought upon himself—he plunged into everything he thought could relate to his duty without a care as to what it might cost him in trouble and sacrifice. In nearly all the incidents related here a more cautious, or less active, or more indolent officer, or one with less self-assurance might have held back, to the delight of Sir Richard Hughes and his fellow occupiers of comfortable berths, although probably not to the benefit of the service.

Even the end of the commission was not peaceful, for the return of the *Boreas* to home waters coincided with the Netherlands dispute, wherein France and Prussia faced each other on the verge of war across the prostrate body of the United Provinces. A France in a better financial condition would have fought, but as it was she had to yield; experience had already taught her that although she might face war with England alone, war against England in alliance with a power-ful Continental state was too exhausting and too perilous. But the danger persisted for several months, during which the *Boreas* was kept in commission and fully engaged upon the task of finding men for the Royal Navy by the process of intercepting merchant ships in the Channel and seizing the bulk of their crews. Pitt had been in power for some time now, and his whole-hearted policy of reducing expenses had been bad for the navy—it was likely that the number of ships available for immediate service was smaller than that at the disposal of France, without considering any accession of strength France could look to from her allies. The condition of the English army at this period was too lamentable for dis-cussion and certainly too lamentable for the army to carry any weight in the settlement of affairs.

We can find in Nelson's correspondence no trace of dis-taste for the press-gang work upon which he was engaged: on the contrary, the activity and ingenuity it called for suited him admirably. It came to an end with the settlement of the dispute in the manner desired by Prussia and England and the turning of French attention to internal rather than to external affairs. In November, 1787, the navy was demobi-lized (if an expression of such technical significance can be applied to a process so floundering as occurred in those days) and the *Boreas* was paid off. A commission crammed with incident had come to an end. What was possibly the most important incident has not yet been noticed; it deserves the distinction of a new chapter.

CHAPTER IV

THE MARRIAGE

AT the height of the altercation at Nevis, when a large body of public opinion on the island was clamouring for Nelson's arrest, and while Nelson was the most hated man within a thousand miles, there were a few prominent people who approved of his motives, if not of his actions, and offered him sympathy and support. The most distinguished of these was a Mr Herbert, a man of some wealth and also President of the Council of the island, who assured him of his sympathy by the very practical method of offering to go bail for him in the event of his arrest.

Nelson had made a profound impression upon Herbert and his family—partly by the manner in which he went out of his way to do his duty, and partly by his extraordinary habit of not drinking more than was good for him at dinner. At the time of his coming into contact with the family Nelson was lonely and unhappy. His enforcement of the Navigation Acts had rendered him unpopular with the civilians and civil servants; his Admiral had no reason to love him; and Mrs Moutray had gone home. Several times he had been on terms of close friendship, if nothing more, with women—the list begins with Lady Parker and continues with the unknown woman in Quebec for whom (according to the badly authenticated story) he nearly gave up the service, Miss Andrews at

St Omer, various fair ladies of Bath, the damsel with whom
he was riding at Portsmouth when the *Boreas* was first commissioned, and ended at present with Mrs Moutray, for
whom it was time a successor was appointed.

Mr Herbert had a widowed daughter almost exactly
Nelson's age, who had married a Dr Nisbet, also of Nevis,
and who had found herself a penniless widow with one son a
year after marriage. Despite the survival of letters written by
her and to her and about her, she remains only a shadowy figure after the most painstaking research. The most salient
feature of her opinions, the one that comes readiest to the
mind, is her belief in the efficacy of flannel worn next the
skin. It is significant that Nelson, who wrote about most
things in terms of superlative, never wrote in such fashion to
or about his wife. To his brother he writes, 'Her manners are
Mrs Moutray's'—not a violent expression of praise, and possibly not one that would have delighted Mrs Nisbet. To herself he writes, 'Real love and esteem is, I trust, what you will
believe I possess in the strongest degree towards you'. That
is not unusual phraseology for an English love-letter of the
year of grace 1785, but it is most unusual for Nelson. His
official reports to the Admiralty breathe more fire and life
than that. Perhaps Prince William—not an exceedingly keen-
witted man—guessed right when he told Nelson that 'he
must have a great esteem for her, and not what is vulgarly
called love'; Nelson certainly agreed with him. At the
moment he had no use for love, even while he fretted when
duty kept the *Boreas* away from Nevis and while he wrote
that he was anxiously awaiting the wedding day. Six months'
tepid courtship saw them betrothed and an allowance
promised him by his uncle, William Suckling, and fifteen
months later they were married, Prince William giving the
bride away.

Nelson's letters after the event do not bubble with happiness. He seems to have entered into the condition of marriage after calm reflection, of the sort he brought to bear upon the study of naval tactics, but (unfortunately, it is to be supposed) the brilliance and the inspiration and the skill which came to him in action did not appear in counterpart in his dealings with his wife. He lost, in fact, very little time in telling his wife that in conditions promising activity he would much prefer to be employed at sea to being on land with her; a little less truth and common sense and a little more illusion and romance would not have appeared out of place, five months after marriage. In his relations with his wife, in fact, Nelson seems to have made no allowance for those things which he would have thought it an affectation to term 'moral imponderabilia', but which he generally reckoned upon most successfully. It is hard to understand why, if he never succeeded in forming an idealized view of his wife, he ever married her, and, conversely, how he ever managed to refrain from idealizing his wife after marrying her. Conceivably flannel next to skin may convey part of the explanation; there are some women whom one cannot idealize, and it is as well to remember that for several years after marriage Nelson lived with his wife in the distasteful inactivity of half-pay in circumstances of unpleasant monotony. A woman who could keep that restless mind happy during years of professional disfavour would have had to have been a woman of an intelligence and an instinctive intuition far above the average. Whether or not Nelson would have accomplished more than he actually did had Mrs Nelson been of this class is a more difficult question still, and it is rather to be thought not, unless the matter is considered by one who holds the opinion that it was on Lady Hamilton's account that Nelson later disobeyed Keith's orders.

It is not a matter of cause and effect, but one of pure co-
incidence, that Nelson vanishes from history for five years
following his marriage. He was out of employment and, as he
was passing his time in England with his wife, in the company
of his father and brother, and in frequent contact with
Captain Locker, his correspondence is very scanty during this
period. It is hard to trace his movements, even, and impossible to find record of his activities. We know that upon more
than one occasion he applied for a ship and was refused, and
we know that once or twice he was threatened by a revival of
the old lawsuits over his action in the islands, but that is all
we know about him. There are stories of his utter discontent
with the service, and of his fury against the Admiralty for
their unwillingness to employ him, but the authority for
these stories is unknown, and most certainly Nelson did not
spend five years in a state of continual fury. What he did in
the intervals can only be an object of guess-work.

Various explanations have been put forward to account for
the Admiralty's omission to employ him. Undoubtedly
Nelson's attitude regarding the West Indian dockyard frauds
would bring upon him the enmity of powerful interests. His
close friendship with Prince William, now become Duke of
Clarence, might have been to his disadvantage, for Clarence
had shown himself to be headstrong and undisciplined,
while politically he had gone over to the Prince of Wales's
Opposition, and his endorsement of Nelson's application
(we know that he did put in a word for Nelson with Hood)
might easily have done more harm than good. The suggestion is even put forward that there was a quarrel between
Hood and Nelson, and rather hazy evidence is advanced to
this effect.

Yet it all seems very unnecessary. Nelson was still a very
junior Captain, and, with only six months' interval, he had

been in employment for over eight years. Pitt had reduced
the navy's numbers as far as any man could dare. There
were numerous captains with records far more distinguished
than Nelson's also seeking their share of the small amount
of employment that was open. It seems hardly more than
natural that he should be left out, and from what we
know of Nelson it is equally natural that he should look on
this inevitable omission as deliberate neglect. If we accept
the fact that Clarence's influence was negligible, we find
that Nelson was without friends of the right kind. Friends in
the service he might have in numbers, but in time of peace
and economy it is political friends who are of most use to a
man in Nelson's position, and as far as we can trace he had
none of any power. Certainly we have Nelson's own
declaration that his collateral descent (on his mother's side)
from the Walpoles never did him a ha'p'orth of good. It has
already been pointed out, too, that Nelson's behaviour on
the Leeward Islands station was not such as to make
Admirals who desired peaceful enjoyment of authority
clamour for his services, however much they might desire
them in time of war. Certainly there seems to be no necessity to assume a quarrel with Hood for an explanation of
Nelson's lack of employment: Hood's later behaviour makes
it unlikely.

So that from December, 1787, to January, 1793, Nelson
remained in England, staying in Bath, in London, and in
Norfolk. His various applications for a ship, including one
made at the time of the Nootka Sound crisis with Spain, had
been unsuccessful. But during all this time the condition of
France had been drifting from bad to worse. Well-meaning
Louis XVI had been weak when he should have been strong,
and strong only when strength brought unpopularity. The
autocrats of Europe had eyed the developments uneasily,

although Pitt had resolved not to make the political condition of France a cause of war between the countries. But both
foreign aggression and internal influences tended to force
France into a condition of hostility towards England, and in
England a powerful and growing party was clamouring for
English intervention in France. One stage followed another,
until at last Pitt whole-heartedly flung aside his peace policy
and made ready for war as lavishly as before he had in miserly
fashion exploited the blessings of peace. The militia was
called out and the navy made ready. There was employment
now for every naval officer, especially for those who had displayed themselves as energetic, thoughtful and fearless of
responsibility.

Three weeks after the Convention had declared itself the
enemy of kings of all kinds Nelson was told that he could
have a seventy-four gun-ship as soon as it was ready; if he did
not feel inclined to wait he could have a sixty-four gun-ship
at once. Did Nelson ever feel inclined to wait? Not when
waiting was of no advantage to the service. He accepted the
offer eagerly, and that is why the name of the sixty-four gun-
ship *Agamemnon* is now so famous, for it was to the *Agamemnon*
that he was appointed two days before the declaration of war
against England by France.

CHAPTER V

THE ENEMY

ENGLAND was entering upon a war which circumstances ensured should be largely naval at a time when sea power was at once more effective and less effective than it later became. The mightiest weapon of sea power, the blockade, could cause a nation an enormous amount of immediate inconvenience. The prevention of the transport of goods by sea meant over a large area the prevention of the transport of goods at all. It would be weeks before goods at Amsterdam, say, would become available for use at Brest. The refitting of a damaged fleet at an ill-supplied harbour in Spain would be impossible of achievement overland from France. A seaboard town without inland water connections would be hard put to to keep itself supplied if the use of the sea were denied to it. The revolution which railways were to make in this connection was as yet undreamed of.

But at the same time the prevention of transport by sea was not such an easy matter as it later became to a superior fleet. At the height of the blockade of France there was still a certain amount of coastwise traffic maintained in small vessels creeping, largely by night, from one fortified inlet to another. In 1813, when the British Navy was at the height of its power, we find Wellington complaining of the frequency with which French ships ran into and out of the harbour of the beleaguered San Sebastian, despite the presence of a powerful British squadron and despite the desperate necessity under which Wellington laboured of the immediate capture of the place. Nor was this coasting traffic the only evidence of maritime mercantile activity on the part of the weaker power. It was not very unusual for quite large convoys to succeed in entering or leaving the ports of the blockaded country, and single merchant ships were sufficiently numerous to attract the profitable commission of a fleet of privateers.

Modern conditions, as exemplified in 1914, were totally opposed to this. No German merchant ship willingly made her appearance outside the Baltic after the declaration of war; a week or two was sufficient to sweep the German flag from every other sea. Nevertheless, land transport was sufficiently developed for this not to be an immediately fatal blow to national existence; bulky materials such as grain could be transported from one district to another rapidly enough to avoid the local gluts and famines which plagued France during the wars of the Revolution, while Government supervision of reserves and modern methods of production made the utmost use of the time available. At the same time the demands of modern warfare are so much more complicated, exacting and urgent that the pressure of blockade makes itself more rapidly felt and is more damaging than was the case a century ago, even although demands which can be satisfied with the material available are more quickly satisfied. There is nothing impossible in the notion of damaged German battleships being repaired at Pola in 1915 with materials sent overland from Germany; but quite a casual study of the Peninsular War gives one a clear enough insight into the condition of Spanish roads to realize the enormous difficulty in 1800 of repairing damaged French battleships at

Corunna with materials sent by road. Imagination shrinks from picturing the effort involved in sending a three-decker's main mast along the mountain road through Lugo where Moore marched so painfully.

A damaged fleet forced into a distant port and blockaded there was likely to remain damaged; indeed, with the inevitable depreciation following the passage of time, it was likely to fall into worse and worse material condition, without taking the moral effect into consideration at all. The reward of victory was therefore proportionately greater, and the pressure of blockade upon a fleet in port had a positive influence in forcing that fleet to come out and risk an action before the chances against it became greater still, or to attempt to escape to some other port where the difficulties of supply and replacement were not so overwhelming. The considerations which led the Franco-Spanish fleet to leave the safety of Cadiz after its action with Calder off Ferrol did not avail to bring the German fleet to risk action after Jutland.

As in every naval war, a series of defeats and the pinning of its fleets to harbour led the weaker naval power to divert its energies rather to commerce destruction than to attempts against the military navy of its opponents. The long French seaboard in the narrow seas was of great advantage for the purpose; despite her lack at that time of Channel harbours suitable for a fleet, there were several bases for privateers, which could count with fair certainty upon escaping to a French port after a blow at English shipping. Especially in the West Indies, but largely in European waters too, attacks were made on merchant ships by large rowboats full of men, whose oars gave them a similar sort of advantage over sailing ships of war as the submarine enjoyed in 1916. The war on commerce was foiled, just as it was later, by the employment of the convoy system, which had been so frequently in use during the last century and a half that one could have expected merchant captains to be both reconciled and accustomed to it; we find, all the same, that they disliked the system—a great many of them did, at any rate—and did not readily adapt themselves to it, so that Parliamentary authority had to be obtained to make it an offence for ships to sail without convoy. We find Nelson writing 'They behaved, as all convoys that I ever saw did, shamefully ill'. The enforcement of rules of convoy (despite the arguments against it, largely identical with those brought forward in 1917) increased the privateers' difficulties enormously, and the same conditions arose as in the case of the Scandinavian convoy in October, 1917, whereby the raiders were tempted (or compelled) to increase the attacking force, and the English to increase the convoying force, until small fleet actions were possible. Moreover, wherever there was a chance of a battleship interfering with convoys, arrangements had to be made to keep that ship neutralized, this neutralization inevitably calling for the employment of a superior force (as the *Goeben* occupied the attention of two battle-cruisers at the Dardanelles). We find a stray French ship of the line at Cadiz causing infinite disturbance, by her mere presence, to Nelson's careful arrangements for convoy in the Mediterranean in 1804.

Command of the sea is demonstrated as much by the use of the ocean highways as by their denial to the enemy, and the responsibility for the protection of merchant shipping was usually the greatest part of the burden of an English naval officer, and, although a victory at sea might lighten it, it could not remove it altogether. That, however, constitutes no argument in favour of the avoidance of victory.

The fleet which England was sending forth in 1793 was going to meet an enemy whose efficiency had been greatly impaired by recent events. The corps of officers which had been built up with so much care by Choiseul was depleted by emigration, although not too much stress should be laid upon this depletion. The career of Villeneuve, whom Nelson fought at Trafalgar, was no more distinguished for rapid promotion than was Nelson's or any one of several other English flag-officers. The belief that victory could be obtained without battles was still current despite (or perhaps because of) the lesson of the American War of Independence. In material the French Navy was not as well supplied as it might be, thanks to the financial mismanagement of earlier years, although the English Navy had at first the same complaint to make after Pitt's fury of economy. The capture of Toulon and the prompt blockade of the French coasts tended, all the same, to maintain this French deficiency. Even after the establishment of the Empire there was complaint in the French Navy that some French ships were not yet fitted with the carronades and gun-mounting improvements which had proved their worth in the English service as far back as the Battle of the Saints.

It was in the quality of the crews that the French Navy was the most inferior. The loss of many officers was partly responsible for this, and the indiscipline resulting from the influence of the Revolution was another factor. Their peace-time training seemingly had been poor, too, and prolonged stay in port after the declaration of war accentuated the fault. The supply of recruits from the merchant service was smaller than in England; moreover, with the disappearance in large part of the French flag from the seas the supply came to an end. In the case of the British Navy a certain proportion of the recruits throughout the war had already had experience at

sea. The encouragement by the French Government of privateering was a severe blow; the best of the French seamen contrived to enter the privateering service, and there, even if
they succeeded in avoiding incarceration in an English prison,
they acquired ideas of discipline and performance very
unsuitable to a seaman of a ship of the line.

This combination of circumstances rather simplified
British strategy without freeing it from any of the guiding
principles. An English ship or an English fleet could be relied
upon to defeat a French ship or fleet of equal force, so that a
distribution which ensured such an encounter could be considered satisfactory, if not brilliant. With even chances, an
English fleet could be reasonably expected to make better
progress over a long voyage than a French one, so that not so
much allowance need be made, if other conditions were
pressing, for the inestimable chances of war.

One other factor must be borne in mind. The control of
the French Navy by landsmen, during both the Revolution
and the Empire, tended to lead to unsound strategy and to a
disregard of the need for training. When we find Napoleon
winning the Battle of Marengo with an army largely com-
posed of recruits who, three weeks before the battle, had had
no musketry training and were doubtful as to which eye to
use to aim, we can understand his belief in an extemporized
fleet and his lack of sympathy with Villeneuve's troubles.
And a study of a few of the schemes seriously considered by
the Committee of Public Safety and by the Directory
enables us to view the colossal error of the expedition to
Egypt with surprise only that it was no worse. In the most
recent European war the influence of the landsmen in the
German Government was generally on the side of inaction,
and the German Navy generally was handled by men who
had made a prolonged, if not profound, study of history, so

that mistakes resulting in immediate crushing punishment were not to be expected; although as a demonstration of what could be devised by a landsman's mind may be cited the action of the French Government, before the English declaration of war, in sending five armoured cruisers to the Straits of Dover with orders to stop the movement into the Channel of the dozen dreadnoughts which the Germans had at their disposal.

It is to be admitted that the German fleet was a highly trained and well-organized body, directed by men of distinguished talents and force of character and they had the advantage over those who directed the course of the French Revolutionary wars in having the history of the French Revolutionary wars as a lesson ever before them. That lesson was taken so much to heart that errors of the one kind were avoided so carefully that errors of the other kind were inevitable; although it would appear on the surface that when opposed to odds of three to two any action or inaction may be written down as an error. To strike a just balance between pedantry and amateurishness, to distinguish between head-strong recklessness and prompt valour and then between caution and overcaution, between patience and irresolution, between conviction and prejudice, are tasks enough to overtry most minds. If, in addition, demand is made for ingenuity, energy and resolution, there are few who can satisfy it. The man who does is the man who makes history for others to read, and write. It calls for a Nelson to create a Nelson tradition, but it also calls for a Nelson to revivify one.

CHAPTER VI

THE PATH OF GLORY

HOOD was destined for the Mediterranean with fifteen ships of the line; there were twenty-one French in Toulon, but numerical superiority was assured by the assistance of the Spanish fleet. The *Agamemnon* was ready for service by April, 1793, manned in large part by Norfolk men attracted by Nelson's personal popularity and recruited by parties sent over by Nelson from Sheerness, but a considerable proportion was contributed by the Chatham guardship—the result of a press, in other words. It was not until the middle of May that Hood's fleet was ready for service, and not until the very end of June that Hood was in his station off Toulon. Pitt's earlier economy and the absence of mobilization plans had much to answer for: privateers backed by battleships had already glutted French harbours with English prizes.

The eternal problem of how to induce an inferior fleet safe in port to come out and be destroyed promptly confronted the allies. They adopted the invariable plan of blockade and waited for things to happen. The French, with discipline nearly at an end, and short of every necessary, could do nothing. The Spanish fleet bore the strain of cruising for sixty days, and then had to return to port to refit and to land their sick, much to Nelson's amusement. His experience with

English crews had taught him that sixty days at sea was just sufficient to settle the men to their duty and to weed out sickness from them.

And then, during the absence of the Spaniards, events moved with a rush. The blockade had done its work, especially after a visit of the fleet to Genoa had convinced that republic that it would be well not to attempt to carry on an organized trade by sea with France. Food ran short in Provence—the district did not grow nearly enough for its own needs—and the excesses of the coming Terror were already expected and feared after the fall of the Gironde. Discontent was general throughout provincial France; here in the south it was augmented by famine and encouraged by the presence of a hostile fleet. The central Government decided on repression and acted vigorously on the decision. The red terror pushed down the valley of the Rhone, Marseilles fell before it, and the guillotine set to work. To save herself from similar outrages, Toulon declared for Louis XVII and admitted the English to the harbour, putting fleet and arsenal in her power. The Spaniards returned in the nick of time to share in the triumph (Hood had carried on the negotiations), and it seemed for the moment as if the Revolution were definitely checked.

But to hold Toulon against a powerful land army troops were needed in numbers; the landing parties Hood and Langara could provide were barely sufficient to man the harbour forts. The Revolution had declared war upon kings; it remained to be seen whether the kings would reply to the challenge with energy. Hood had to send some one instantly to find out, and the man he sent was one not of his two Admirals, nor one of his five senior Captains. It was Nelson—and the choice was a clear proof of Hood's sound ability in the distinguishing of talent. Off went Nelson. He

made urgent appeal to the King of Sardinia, hardly stayed a
moment, and rushed on to Naples. Here Sir William
Hamilton was the Minister of the English Government, and
with him was his wife, the lovely Emma, whom he had just
married after living with her for a number of years. But for
her Nelson had no time to spare at present: to him she was
just 'a young woman of amiable manners, who does honour to
the station to which she is raised'. Hamilton was the person
he wanted to communicate with, and through him with the
King and the Prime Minister—Sir John Acton, that strange
character, seventh baronet, Italian born of English parentage,
Italian trained, supple, talented, not too trustworthy, politically a reactionary when not opportunist, late Minister of
Marine and of War at Naples, now Prime Minister, soon to be
Generalissimo on Land and Sea of the Neapolitan forces, and
eventually father and grandfather of two of the most profound and respected English thinkers of the nineteenth century. The news of the fall of Toulon, of the beginning of the
end of the Revolution, thrilled Naples, delighted Hamilton
and Acton. Bourbon Ferdinand's attention was diverted from
his slaughter of game to the business of the nation. Nelson
had three interviews with him on shore, and received him
once on board the *Agamemnon*, with Hamilton and Acton to
interpret. Such was Nelson's influence on the three of them
that in four days Ferdinand had not merely promised assistance, but promptly allocated six thousand men for service at
Toulon and actually set going the machinery for their immediate despatch—promptitude which finds few counterparts
in Neapolitan history.

Nelson did not remain to convoy these troops, which he
had obtained by anticipating Hood's further instructions.
News arrived of a French frigate on the Italian coast. He
dashed out after her, only four days after his arrival, found

her in Leghorn harbour, and left her there when he found there was no possibility of her quitting neutral water while he was in attendance. He was back at Toulon by October 5th, and found the Neapolitan troops already arrived, proof of the success of this his first detached command—first of a series which was to extend with few breaks up to the Peace of Amiens.

A fortnight later he was sent off again to accompany Commodore Linzee to Tunis, and on the way the *Agamemnon* encountered a squadron of four French frigates. Hotly pursuing one of them during the hours just before and after dawn, *Agamemnon* had her rigging badly cut up by her, because, cleverly handled, she made use of her superior speed to yaw and deliver broadsides at intervals, while only *Agamemnon*'s bow guns could bear. The damage enabled the frigate to join her consorts, and after contemplating each other for a while, both sides were glad to separate without further fighting. The incident is notable because Nelson called a council of war to deliberate on whether he was justified in not renewing the contest; the council of war, bearing out Napoleon's saying, decided that he was. In Nelson's case the summoning of the council was a wise precaution, because no English naval officer could dare to avoid action without very good reason, and he might have needed justification in the eyes of his Commander-in-Chief.

Joining Linzee at Cagliari, *Agamemnon* went on with him to Tunis, where Linzee, in accordance with instructions, sent in to ask permission to attack a French ship of the line and convoy which were lying there (the frigates Nelson had just encountered had been on their way from Tunis too). Permission was refused, and the English had the mortification of seeing a valuable convoy and a fighting ship lying within their reach in what was practically a piratical

stronghold and yet not being able to touch it. Nelson would
have gone in and taken them, and given the Bey a share of
the plunder to compensate for the injury to his dignity. It
might have proved a sound plan; success would certainly
have made the Bey England's accomplice and therefore her
ally. But Linzee was tied by his instructions; and it is a risky
business attacking a fortified port with ships alone. Failure
would certainly have made an enemy of the Bey, and that
meant far more damage to England than the loss of the
convoy would have been to France. Once negotiations had
been opened it was most likely better to abide by their
result. What Nelson wanted to do was to lay hold of the
convoy first and negotiate afterwards. He had a very clear
idea of the value of a *fait accompli*.

But another detached command relieved Nelson of the
burden of Linzee's presence. *Agamemnon* was ordered back to
Corsica, there to look after the frigates she had recently
encountered, and to assist a small squadron to blockade the
ports of the place. In addition, Nelson was to enforce a blockade of Genoa; as usual, the stronger power at sea had lost
patience with the evasions of the weaker neutrals, and was
enforcing her rulings with a strong hand. Nelson, to whom all
this important duty was assigned, had five captains senior to
him present with Hood—'a very high compliment', he wrote.

And then, calling at Leghorn for provisions, Nelson saw a
number of ships and small vessels come into the port. They
bore cargoes of misery. Some of them were full of wounded
soldiers from Toulon, but for the most part they were packed
with civilians, men, women and children, utterly destitute,
'families without fathers, and fathers without families', all
fleeing from the red terror which had burst into Toulon.

The defence had been carried on by French, English,
Spanish, Piedmontese and Neapolitan troops. The most

numerous contingent had been the Spaniards, and the
Spaniards were wearying of the English alliance. They had
far less wish to see England dominant in the Mediterranean
than France; French action in Catalonia had frightened
them; they were nettled by the typically English assumption
of superiority in naval matters; and the troops they had sent
had been shockingly bad. Ill will between English and
Spaniards rose to such a height that there had been a significant hauling of cables and pointing of guns in Toulon harbour. The town itself was full of French sympathizers. The
most of the population hated their protectors only less than
they hated the Paris Government. Against this motley horde
of five nations, divided against itself, riddled with intrigue,
badly supplied and worse led, Paris sent a homogeneous
army, and ensured the activity of its commander by the presence of her own representatives and the appalling threat of
the guillotine. More than that, Paris sent Bonaparte. Violent
attacks by the National army, directed on the vital point by
Bonaparte, decided the fate of the wretched city. On the
16th of December Bonaparte's guns commanded the
entrance to the port. There was no hope of retaking the key
of the town with the miserable troops at hand, and evacuation was all that could be decided upon. The ships which
were ready sailed crammed with refugees; the allied troops
were hurried on board their transports, and as they embarked
the National army poured in, and the guillotine was to follow
them. There were thirty French ships of the line in harbour
there, and an immense quantity of naval stores, which ought
to have been destroyed before the allies quitted the place;
but Spanish ill will (it might be more correct to write
Spanish bad faith) and the suddenness of the turn of events
hampered the work of destruction. The evacuation of civilians, too, occupied some of the attention of the English, and

the rapid entrance of the National troops saved much where destruction had already been begun. From believing in the almost total destruction of the French Navy at Toulon the English came gradually to realize that both ships and stores had been nearly all spared. Five thousand, at least, of the crews had earlier escaped from the town and joined the National forces, so that it was only very soon after the allied evacuation of Toulon that a French fleet was assembled there, to plague the English by the constant menace of its presence. Such was the miserable end of a miserable venture: their counterparts can almost exactly be found in the history of the exploits of Koltchak and Denikin a hundred odd years later.

Nelson sent to the Admiralty such news of the disaster as he could gather at Leghorn, and proceeded again to Corsica, where, after being blown off again by a gale, he found, to his irritation, that one of the frigates blockaded at San Fiorenzo had succeeded in making her way along to Calvi with provisions. The latter place had been so straitened by the blockade up to this time that it was on the point of surrender—an interesting sidelight on the internal communications of Corsica. All the same, assistance was close at hand. Hood's squadron was on its way from Toulon, and with it came the two or three thousand troops which constituted the British striking force in the Mediterranean. The self-same gale which had blown Nelson away scattered the English fleet, and there was much further delay in consequence before the English forces were gathered together again for the attack on the island.

The provision of an advanced base for the Mediterranean squadron was a matter of urgency. Hood made use for a brief space of Hyères Bay, but there was no hope of remaining there in presence of the French army. Minorca, it might be supposed, would be at the disposition of Spain's allies, but Spain was not too trustworthy, and for some purpose Corsica would be the best possible base. Incidentally, the conquest of Corsica would rob France of a province and reduce the number of refuges for privateers and fighting ships—the four frigates *Agamemnon* had fought were in her harbours ready to fall as prizes into the hands of the conquerors. The deciding factor was the present opposition to French rule. Paoli had been allowed to return at the Revolution, and, dissatisfied, like many of his countrymen, with the further progress of events, he had countenanced and headed rebellion against the central authority. Sea power had been a powerful factor; troops could not reach the island from the mainland, with the result that the rebels, half-hearted and divided in sentiment though they were, had succeeded in clearing the interior and in penning the loyalists into the seaboard towns. Mainly through Paoli's influence the sovereignty of the island had been offered to, and accepted by, George III. Hood brought in his fleet a man of most distinguished ability, Sir Gilbert Elliot, as Viceroy. The English rule of Corsica was begun under the happiest auspices.

While Nelson menaced Bastia and kept that place in a state of alarm, Hood's main squadron appeared in San Fiorenzo Bay. The troops were promptly landed, and the two French frigates there surrendered to this overwhelming force. Hood and Nelson had taken it for granted that the next step would be an immediate attack upon Bastia—a dozen miles away over a low mountain range—but Dundas, commanding the army, decided against it. There were over four thousand men in arms in Bastia, and the place was fortified well enough to call for a formal siege for its capture. Dundas, with fourteen hundred men, was not going to make the attempt. He came up to the place and went away again,

to the disgust of the fleet. It must be remembered in his
favour into what condition the English army had fallen in
1794; incidentally also must it be remembered that officials
in London had the care-free habit (which reached its climax
in the Crimea) of sending British expeditionary forces by sea
without any transport and even without horses, and expecting them to be able to march and fight on arrival. They
generally fought well enough, but to march any distance was
beyond their power. Dundas distrusted his Corsican allies,
and, with meticulous military sense, he denounced the siege
of a place with a garrison thrice the strength of the besiegers
as an impracticable operation—'a most visionary and rash
attempt' are his very words. What he did not allow for,
thereby displaying himself as an educated soldier with no
spark of genius, was the moral condition of the garrison of
Bastia, cut off for months from communication with France,
hemmed in by insurgents whose ferocity they knew and
whose strength they exaggerated, with a disaffected civilian
population all round them, and, most important of all, not
too much attached to the cause for which they were fighting.

Hood attached weight to these factors, Nelson more still;
on his own confession he did not give his Commander-in-
Chief all the information in his possession regarding the
strength of the garrison, fearing that if he did so Hood might
incline to Dundas's opinion. The upshot of the argument
was that the navy washed its hands of the army, which it left
at San Fiorenzo, and proceeded to the siege of Bastia with
the troops at its own disposal (regular infantry employed on
board as marines) and a small landing party of seamen; for
siege materials and mortars Hood sent to borrow from the
Neapolitan Government.

Once determined upon, the siege was pushed with all the
vigour and energy to be expected when Nelson held a com-

mand. The blockade by sea was so effective that all efforts to throw in reinforcements and supplies from the neighbouring mainland failed completely. A battery was thrown up on shore at a spot determined upon by Nelson—his choice was approved by an artillery and an engineer officer from the San Fiorenzo troops—and approaches were begun. The inevitable friction between soldiers and seamen was reduced to a minimum by the tact of Hood and Nelson. By the time the batteries opened on the land side, gunboats bombarded the place by night from the sea, and garrison and population were unremittingly harassed. Supplies were short and disaffection grew apace. At the beginning of May Nelson was writing to his wife in confidence about secret information in his possession of the approaching fall of the place; he was even able to name the date fairly exactly, which he certainly would not have been able to do without an understanding with the garrison, or at least without very good friends within the fortification.

Shortness of supplies and the harassing siege operations drove the garrison to open negotiations. Meanwhile General d'Aubant, who had succeeded Dundas in command of the expeditionary force, so far allowed his opinions to change that instead of 'not entangling himself in any co-operation' (his own words), he marched his men towards the place. They made their appearance on the heights above the town at the psychological moment that negotiations were begun, and the place surrendered. Military opinion, including that even of him who later became Sir John Moore of the march to Corunna, was proved incorrect, and Hood and (much more particularly) Nelson were justified.

Calvi was now the only place in Corsica remaining to the French, and the decision was promptly made to attack it, this time with the cordial co-operation of the army, now under

General Stuart—not the John Stuart who won the Battle of
Maida, but Charles Stuart, a man of much more genius and
resolution. In the midst of the embarkation of the stores for
the siege came the news that the Toulon fleet, which had
nominally been destroyed at the evacuation, was out in force
apparently superior to the inshore blockading squadron.
Hotham, commanding the latter, fled precipitately to Calvi
before numbers which were later found to be no greater
than his own. Hood hurried to the rendezvous, *Agamemnon*
caught him up on the way, having taken only half an
hour extra to unload two hundred tons of ordnance, and
before the superior force thus assembled the French retired
again to their own coast. Hotham for months afterwards was
to experience the inconvenience resulting from his refusal to
engage when he had the chance; it is not to be imagined that
he regretted it, because seemingly to his dying day he did
not appreciate the blessedness of an opportunity of action
with a blockaded fleet.

Long before the French were out of harm's way Hood sent
back *Agamemnon* to recommence the preparation against
Calvi, and Nelson showed what he thought (when it came to
his own practice) of the theory of the 'fleet in being' by
transporting the stores round to Calvi and starting to land
them, believing himself, correctly enough, to be 'safe under
his lordship's wing'. Calvi was a place of very considerable
strength, and the only landing-place near not commanded by
its guns—it had to be near, what with the badness of the
roads and the want of transport in the army—was exceedingly bad. Good seamanship, however, got the guns and
stores on shore, and Nelson's endless energy got them into
position. The siege was pressed with vigour, although never
fast enough to suit Nelson's impatience nor Hood's anxiety.
The Toulon fleet was slowly but steadily increasing in

numbers with the refitting of some ships and the building of others. Soon Hood would have to call away the troops and seamen belonging to the ships in order to be ready to fight at a moment's notice. Malaria and all the diseases which plague troops in trenches were showing themselves in the ranks. Of all the operations of war on land a siege presents to the inexperienced onlooker the most apparently senseless delays, although there is none more certain of success if outside influences are kept away. The time spent on methodical approaches seemed wasted to Nelson, who more than once wrote to Hood announcing the immediate storm of an outwork several days before the stormers deemed an assault advisable; and in the motley besieging force news of this kind leaked out (probably by way of Corsican members of Hood's or Elliot's staffs), much to Stuart's annoyance. Sharp letters passed backwards and forwards between the fleet, the landing party and the soldiers; but all sides kept their tempers and trouble was avoided.

At the same time, Nelson began to fret about the wording of Hood's official report on the taking of Bastia. There had been an agreement between him and Hood that a Captain Hunt, who had recently lost his ship and whom Hood was anxious to put in a favourable light before the official eye, should have favourable mention, but, when Nelson found that Hood had attributed to Hunt (who had been under his orders) the whole glory of the command of the batteries, and had left Nelson only the mediocre distinction of the successful landing of stores, he not unnaturally complained that Hood had overstepped the limits of what a man should do for a friend. His discontent, however, only found vent in bitter complaints in private letters, and in a note to his wife we find the philosophic utterance, 'Never mind, one day I shall have a Gazette to myself'. The relations between Hood and

Nelson remained cordial until Hood soon after went home ill.

On 12th July Nelson was struck in the face by a shower of
stones and sand thrown up by a shot hitting the parapet of his
battery. He was much bruised, and the sight of his right eye
was destroyed, but he did not allow the injury to keep him
out of action even for a day. He sent no word of it to his wife
until August 18th, when he broke the news to her gently but
with a baldness of phrasing characteristic of these letters; he
drew consolation from the fact that he could still see quite
well with the other eye. He says next to nothing about any
pain or distress caused by the wound, neither to his wife nor
to anyone else. In the midst of the activities of a siege he was
not likely to give much thought to physical pain.

Calvi, despite the fortunate arrival of various small vessels
which eluded the blockading squadron, would not stand an
assault. The fall of the outworks and the opening of the batteries upon the main defences convinced the garrison that
further defence was useless, and after a good deal of negotiation the place capitulated on August 10th, and the fleet was
free to leave that malaria-ridden stretch of waste and try to
recruit the health of its shattered crews. Eight days after the
surrender the *Agamemnon* was in Leghorn, there to enjoy a
month's rest after eighteen months' continuous active service.

England was free now to try to capture the affections of
the Corsicans, and the English fleet, having, after a year's
hard fighting, secured itself a base, was able to turn its attention to operations on the mainland in addition to maintaining its unceasing watch over the Toulon fleet.

CHAPTER VII

AGAMEMNON

THE rebellion of Toulon had marked the lowest point in the fortunes of the new republic, and the year 1794 had witnessed a steady recovery. By the end of the year France had practically put an end to internal revolt, and had spread her conquests to her 'natural boundaries'. Spain, Tuscany, Prussia, had all made peace with her or were obviously on the point of doing so. A powerful body of opinion in France was in favour of a general peace. The party in power inclined rather to a policy of aggression, and were supported in this by the continued enmity of England and Austria. At sea one great battle had been fought, the glorious First of June, wherein Lord Howe had tried to counter the traditional tactics of the French Navy by the rather risky method of breaking the French line with every ship simultaneously and engaging from to-leeward. His plan had not met with complete success: some of his Captains had not displayed all the ingenuity and energy required, the French had fought hard, and Lord Howe, either from force of circumstances or from an error of judgment, did not wring every possible profit from his success. The capture or destruction of half a dozen ships of the line was the sole fruit of victory. The convoy of grain ships whose approach to the French coast had brought on the battle had reached France safely and relieved

a critical situation in the matter of food supplies, and the
desperate fighting of the *Vengeur*, as described in the lying
French official account, put fresh heart into the French people regarding the possibilities of a naval war. The French
Government came to decisions of extreme ferocity. It
decreed that no prisoners were to be taken at sea, and actually perpetrated at least one small massacre (of the crew of a
small English vessel taken in the Mediterranean), besides
ordering the employment of devices, such as red-hot shot
and incendiary bombs, which were generally regarded as
uncivilized and contrary to the laws of war at sea—mainly, it
is to be presumed, because they could not be employed
without extreme danger to the user.

In the Mediterranean the situation was governed largely
by two factors. The south of France and the French armies
there depended for food upon sea-borne supplies—the
Corniche road was not very practicable until the Consulate.
To interfere with the coasting ships engaged on this traffic
called for the unremitting attention of an English squadron
operating close inshore, and a not very tender regard for
Genoese neutrality. To counter the efforts of this squadron,
the French needed to occupy the coast and provide fortified
refuges for small ships (assuming, that is to say, that they
were unwilling to use their fleet), and necessarily therefore
completely to ignore Genoese neutrality. The other factor
was the precarious hold of England upon Corsica. The army
of occupation was small, the party in favour of England was
weak, and there was a growing party which was not merely
anti-English but pro-French. A very few thousand French
troops, out of the great number at the disposal of France, if
once landed in Corsica would reconquer the island and
deprive the English fleet of its painfully acquired base. A sufficient force could probably be carried on the ships of the

line in Toulon, without necessitating the employment of transports. That, combined with the annoyance of the coastal blockade, would be a splendid enough bait to induce the Toulon fleet to risk a raid upon Corsica. Napoleon at St Helena later declared that it was a result of his remonstrances that the Toulon fleet did not put to sea, in obedience to orders from Paris, transports and all; but, remembering the conditions of the expedition to Egypt, it would be well not to put too much faith in the statement.

However it was, in March 1795 word came to Hotham (Hood's successor) at Leghorn that the French were out, fifteen ships of the line, and Hotham cleared from the port in desperate haste to head them off, with thirteen British battleships (*Agamemnon* among them) and one Neapolitan. On the morning of the 12th the French were in sight—Nelson and half a dozen others close up to them, the rest of the fleet hull down to leeward. A day of feverish anxiety followed, a day of light baffling winds and mist, but not a shot was fired, for the French declined to try to profit by the opportunity of attacking the nearer English ships. Next day the fleets were still in sight of each other, but the wind was stronger. Hotham flew the signal for a general chase, each ship for himself, compelling the enemy to stand and fight lest his slower ships be overwhelmed by the faster ones among the pursuers.

Nelson's chance was come. For the first time in his life he was in a ship forming part of one of two fleets in presence. So far the engagement of October 1793, between *Agamemnon* and the frigates, had been his only serious action at sea during twenty-five years in the navy. Now he anticipated a fleet action, and *Agamemnon* was the likeliest ship to bring one about. He was to have his reward for holding to her and her crew despite all Hood's offers of larger but slower ships.

Agamemnon was small, fast and handy; good fortune had placed her nearest the French fleet, and Nelson had kept her there. He proceeded to work up to windward, getting every possible yard of progress out of his ship. Already, on the eve of this first fleet action, amid the din of the removal of bulkheads and clearing for action, he had written tenderly to his wife, seemingly under a presentiment of death; now on deck he watched the slow overhauling of the French fleet by *Agamemnon* with impatience. He had noted, the day before, that 'they did not appear to act like officers who knew anything of their profession'. Although he did not know it, one ship of the line had parted company in the night through loss of topmasts in the fresh westerly wind, and now, under his very eye, another ran clumsily into her next ahead and lost fore and main topmasts, being rapidly left behind by the bulk of the French fleet in its flight. Nelson had his opportunity now, and his reward for his diligence. He tacked towards the disabled *Ça Ira*, which was taken in tow, after an hour's delay, by a frigate. Dashing down upon her, nearly isolated as she was—there were only two French ships of the line within gunshot of her—he took the place of an English frigate which had gallantly engaged the battleship and had been beaten off. *Ça Ira* opened desperately with her stern guns in the hope of disabling this new and more powerful pursuer, but Nelson, keeping out of the way of her broadside, came up on her stern, let his ship's head fall off from the wind, and drove his own broadside raking into her stern. Then, coming up to the wind again, he made up for the distance lost, and then repeated the manoeuvre, firing broadside after broadside into the hapless *Ça Ira*'s stern, keeping up his fire for two hours, during which period a hundred and ten men of the *Ça Ira* were killed and wounded, and so much damage was done that fifteen hours later *Ça Ira* still had no topmasts hoisted. *Agamemnon*, be it noted, was a very small ship of the line, *Ça Ira* was an eighty-gun ship and big at that—her weight of metal was twice *Agamemnon*'s—and in a fight broadside to broadside the latter must have been shattered. As it was, she had only seven men wounded. After two hours of this maddening bombardment the frigate succeeded in hauling *Ça Ira* round head to wind so that her broadside would bear, while the other French ships had turned back to save their colleague. One more broadside, and *Agamemnon* turned down wind in obedience to the Admiral's recall; Nelson had done his part, not so much in the damage inflicted on the *Ça Ira* as in interrupting the French retreat. Nelson notes that the old tradition still lingered in the French fleet, as they fired at spars in preference to the hull, and, being bad marksmen, did extraordinarily little damage. *Agamemnon* was in full fighting order again by evening.

Next morning the two fleets were still close together, and between them lay the helpless *Ça Ira*, in tow of a ship of the line, the *Censeur*. A signal from Hotham sent the two nearest English ships into action against them while the rest of the fleet formed line of battle. *Ça Ira* and *Censeur* fought back hard, and soon all four were crippled and motionless, a prize for whichever fleet should be victorious. The French Admiral made up his mind to fight, and came down with the wind. Hotham handled his line clumsily, but he managed to interpose between the French and the disabled ships, of which the French ones received the starboard broadsides of the English fleet, while the port ones were discharged at the main French fleet. The two lines neared each other; it seemed as if they were going to pass along on opposite courses, when the French Admiral's resolution faltered. He turned up into the wind again. The fire was distant and ineffective, and in the English fleet only the leaders got within range, and, subjected to the successive fire of the French line, the first two were seriously crippled.

It seemed to be the moment for the English to tack in hot pursuit; they were at grips at last with the fleet that had caused them so much anxiety and trouble. But the cannonade died away; and the French, abandoning hope of recapturing the two lost ships of the line, made all diligence to get out of harm's way. Nelson, furious at seeing an opportunity passing ungrasped at, rushed on board Hotham's flagship, next astern to *Agamemnon*, and begged him to order pursuit. Hotham refused in mild astonishment. Goodall, second in command, was in *Princess Royal*, next ahead. Nelson rushed to Goodall, and found him in agreement. Still Hotham would not move. 'We have done very well', he said. And there were eleven sail of the enemy's line to the southward untaken!

Nelson actually managed to find excuses for Hotham— and naturally it is a debatable point whether pursuit would have been successful—but from that time on he had no use for his Admiral, and he never ceased regretting that Hood had not been in command on that fatal day. The bitterness increased when it was found that at the beginning of their raid the French had fallen in with and taken an English ship of the line, which had been refitting at San Fiorenzo, and still more when six sail of the line succeeded in reaching Toulon from Brest, thus raising the strength of the Toulon fleet considerably above that of the united English and Neapolitan squadrons, until Man brought out reinforcements. In the interval there was considerable anxiety lest the French might come out once more and force a battle by attacks on Corsica or Naples.

But for three months the English fleet continued to cruise unassailed between Minorca and Italy; Nelson was worried for a space by the fear that the promotions which rewarded the victory of the 1st June, 1794, should give him his flag and take him off the station, but they stopped short seven above him on the list. Furthermore, they made vacant some of the four Colonelcies of Marines, and Nelson was appointed, at George III's special request, it is said, to one of the vacancies. The rank conveyed a fair income with it, so that from this time onward there was no particular reason for him ever to be pressed for money.

Now began a series of detached commands for Nelson. He was sent off with his own ship and some smaller vessels to co-operate with Austrians and Sardinians on the Genoese coast. The primary object of the operations was to force back the French army far enough to allow Vado Bay to be used as a base by the English fleet. The Austrians reached their objective, but before any use could be made of it the French fleet, seventeen of the line, made its appearance, and Nelson had to fly for San Fiorenzo with the enemy in hot pursuit. A little more luck and a little greater skill on the part of the French, and *Agamemnon* might have suffered the fate of the *Berwick*, which had fallen to the French in their last cruise, just as Admiral Beatty and his battle-cruisers nearly fell into German hands one fateful day in December 1914. But *Agamemnon* succeeded in outsailing all seventeen of the French ships of the line, and came safe to San Fiorenzo Bay, where Hotham, who had jumped to the conclusion that the French had come out merely to exercise the men, was mildly surprised to see Nelson and his pursuers. The baffling Mediterranean calms left *Agamemnon* grievously exposed for some hours more before Hotham got out to her help (he had run a most wanton risk in leaving *Agamemnon* unsupported when he knew the French were out), and the following days saw a long, weary chase before light winds and fitful gales back to the French coast. On July 13th the fleets were in sight—so also was the French coast—and Hotham, after wasting time in an endeavour to form line of battle, signalled for a general chase.

Half a dozen of the leading ships got within range of the rearmost French. *Agamemnon* was one of the former, the others being Man's division fresh from England. The distant fire which was all that could be maintained fell mainly on the last French ship, the *Alcide*, which was first crippled, next set on fire, next surrendered, and which finally blew up (a fate which Nelson attributed to the unsportsmanlike combustibles carried in her tops), but the French abandoned her, just as *Blücher* was abandoned at the Dogger Bank, and made good their escape to the protection of the shore batteries. Hotham, eight miles astern, called off his van (prematurely, they say), and the action was over. Once more a French fleet had got away through lack of energy and diligence on the part of an English Admiral. A thorough beating of the French fleet would, as far as it is possible to judge, have saved the evacuation of the Mediterranean which subsequently became necessary, with the loss of Corsica which ensued, and might well have served to keep Spain neutral for a few more important years. It was one more lesson to Nelson on the value of promptitude and resolution, and can be saved as an example to answer charges of rashness which may be brought against his own plans.

With this unsatisfactory end to the interruption, Hotham repeated his orders to Nelson to continue his observation of the Riviera coast. Although Hotham's orders gave Nelson a free hand in the most handsome fashion to do whatever he thought fit for the common cause, with the advice of the Austrian General de Vins, and the English Minister, Drake, at Turin, at the same time he restricted Nelson most grievously by a simultaneous order, drawn up in agreement with instructions from London, to be most careful in his dealings with neutral shipping lest he give offence to neutral powers.

Nelson on his arrival found that there was an extensive trade between France on the one hand and Genoa and Tuscany on the other; moreover, this trade was of the utmost importance to the French army on the Riviera; and the only form of co-operation with the Austrians open to the English fleet was the interference with this traffic. The Austrians, like the members in their argument with the belly, and in the manner of all allies, were convinced that they were doing more than their fair share of the work. Their urgent appeal to Nelson, endorsed by Drake's arguments, decided him to act once more against orders and convince Austria of England's goodwill. He had to take his 'political courage' in both hands to do so, however; Hotham kept himself carefully out of the way—co-operation with forces on land intimidated him—and Nelson alone had the responsibility. If the owners of the vessels he seized sued him for damages and won their case he would be liable for the payment of hundreds of thousands of pounds.

Nelson's action had instant effect; he seized several ships, and the trade came to an end. Insurance rates between Genoa and Marseilles rose to a restrictive figure. Some French ships which took refuge on the Genoese coast under shelter of French batteries were taken or destroyed after warning had been given—Nelson rightly arguing that they could not claim the protection of neutral water when the coast behind them was in an enemy's hands. The unfortunate state of Genoa saw her sovereignty violated by all four contending states, and her outlying towns in distress in consequence of Nelson's blockade, but she herself had erred too far from the straight path of neutrality for her protests

to have much point, and with Nelson hard at hand she
could dare nothing. Nelson's action was upheld by his
Government, and the French army fell into a state of distress
which Napoleon's first general order of the following spring
only describes with moderation.

Various new developments, however, deprived Nelson's
blockade of some of its force and made it just possible for the
French army to exist. Spain made peace the day after
Nelson's arrival on the coast, so that supplies became available from that quarter both by sea and land. The French
troops engaged in the Pyrenees were brought up to reinforce
the army in the Maritime Alps. The coasting trade began
again in very small vessels, which crept along in water too
shallow for Nelson's squadron, and the French established
batteries everywhere along the coast to afford them
protection.

Nelson did all he could. He used his ships' boats against
these coasters; he tried to organize a shallow-draught
squadron; he sent to Naples begging for gunboats. This
request was refused, and the coasting trade continued to survive and maintain itself in just sufficient strength for the
French army to exist. There was one last expedient which
was not tried; Nelson suggested that he should take a division of Austrian troops round behind the French front and
land them on the coast, where they would break the land
communications and at the same time compel the coasters
to come away from the shore at that point and run into the
arms of his waiting cruisers. Vins, probably correctly, refused
to risk a detachment in this fashion. Had there been a
Gibraltar along this piece of coast, and had there been any
chance of seizing it, the plan promised large reward; but, as
it was, such a landing party would have been exposed to
destruction by the superior forces which would have been

hurled upon it immediately, and at best could only hope for a hurried re-embarkation, with all its attendant losses in men and material. Vins held that there was no impregnable position on the coast covering a good landing, and he was most likely right. Nelson quite failed to appreciate the force of the argument, and he was most likely wrong. Vins was a formalist general of the old unenterprising school, but his opinion on a major military operation should be accepted before Nelson's.

Hotham gave up his command to Sir Hyde Parker, and Parker in turn was relieved by Sir John Jervis, the man of iron nerve and phlegmatic courage, the ferocious disciplinarian, the man whose greatest talent was the discernment of talent in others, and whose experience of active service went back to Wolfe's capture of Quebec. But Jervis arrived too late to aid Nelson on the Riviera coast. The battle of Loano had swept the Austrians back into the Apennines, and the coast was lined by now with batteries ready to fling red-hot shot into any English vessel which came in range. Vins had been super-seded by Beaulieu, and Austria was voicing bitter complaints that the disaster of Loano was the fault of the English—a ridiculous plea, but comforting to Austrian national pride. Vado Bay was once more in French hands, and English men of war had to depend on the timorous neutrality of Tuscany for the use of Leghorn. Still, the position of the English fleet was not one of too great difficulty, and Jervis was able to detach Nelson again to the Riviera coast, while he continued to observe Toulon. Nelson was able to write, delightedly, that Jervis treated him more as a colleague than as a subordi-nate—and he knew, too, of the jealousy such distinction roused in the breasts of his fellow captains.

Nelson's main duty now was the prevention of an effort he was firmly convinced would be made by the French—the

despatch of a force by sea against Genoa or Leghorn. He saw
clearly enough the motives for such a movement—the
wealth of Italy was a standing temptation to the starving
French hordes—but, oddly enough, he did not realize the
enormous danger to which the attempt would expose the
army making it. Its departure would weaken the main force;
the detachment would run the risk of destruction should it
encounter the English fleet on the way, and once landed it
would be in an unfriendly country, with no means of communication with France, and liable to be overwhelmed by
the Austrian force acting on interior lines. All the same,
Nelson believed the French would chance it, and preparations made in French ports for the transport of troops and
supplies by sea maintained him in the delusion—the preparations actually being in small part directed against Corsica,
but largely coming into existence as a result of the fortification of the coast and the consequent ease of coastal communication. For a man with a name unknown to Nelson—it
does not creep into his correspondence for some time yet—
had just been appointed to the command of the Army in
Italy, and was gathering his forces together for a spring at his
scattered enemies.

It was while Nelson was watching for the sailing of
this illusory expedition, and pressing upon the Austrian
command his old plan of transporting Austrian troops
round the French seaward flank, that Bonaparte struck.
Montenotte, Dego, Millesimo, the campaign was hall-
marked from the beginning with the Napoleonic characteris-
tics: feints, extension, concentration by forced marches, a
fierce blow, an instant following up of the victory, and utter
disregard of the weariness of the men in the ranks. A fortnight after Montenotte, Nelson was writing dejectedly to
Collingwood that Sardinia was making peace with France.

Bonaparte had opened the rich plains of Lombardy to himself without making use of a perilous eccentric movement by sea. For Nelson remained the dismal task of forwarding to Jervis the news he picked up at Genoa and elsewhere: the news of the French contributions levied on Piedmont, the news of Lodi, the news of the occupation of Milan. So convinced did he become of the completeness with which the French were supplied in Italy that he wrote to Jervis suggesting that his squadron should be recalled, although this might involve his striking the distinguishing pendant Jervis had ordered him to hoist. But before Jervis could act on the suggestion, Nelson had proved the continued need of the presence of his force by the capture, under the guns of the battery at Oneglia, of the siege train destined for Bonaparte's use at Mantua. It was a capture which was destined to cost France dear in blood and money and time—just as the sinking of the Japanese howitzers by the Vladivostock squadron meant the loss of thousands of Japanese lives at Port Arthur—although Bonaparte's untiring energy and fierce resolution were to make the least of the loss.

This was the last achievement for some time of the *Agamemnon*. The old ship was in a bad way—only held together by the cables wrapped round her—and for a space it seemed as if Nelson would have to go to England with her when she sailed for her refit. But Jervis was able to arrange an exchange, and Nelson hoisted his broad pendant on the *Captain*, 74, in June 1796. Nelson was still in doubts as to the permanency of his stay; he was so high on the post list now that his promotion to Rear-Admiral might occur at any moment, and with that might, or most probably would, come his recall to England.

And meanwhile events were moving towards a crisis. With Bonaparte established in the heart of Italy, with a victorious army at his back, the lesser Italian states were at his mercy, and the change in the situation displayed itself in the increasing antagonism of the Italian Governments. Genoa, helpless before the French troops, was so unfriendly that a blockade of Genoa was proclaimed. Tuscany was invaded by a French detachment, and a sudden rush upon Leghorn nearly resulted in the capture of the English shipping there; it only got away in consequence of the exertions of Captain Fremantle. With so much of the Italian coast in their possession, it was far easier for the French to land small parties of men in Corsica, and this they proceeded to do despite Nelson's care, and despite his occupation (by Jervis's and Elliot's orders) of the islands of Capraja and Elba. For a space Nelson planned an attack upon Leghorn by troops brought from Corsica or Naples, but the continued occupation of the town was not a practicable operation (although he seemed to have thought it was), and the next developments were to render it still more impracticable. For the army which had invaded Tuscany pressed on towards the Papal States and Naples, and both these powers, helpless against considerable military force, made their peace with France. And when a minor power finds it necessary to leave an alliance which is at war with another, it generally finds neutrality impossible (as Count Czernin was to plead long afterwards), and must side with its late enemies against its old friends. Italy was now in a state of hostility, latent or active, towards England. Corsica was steadily growing more and more restive under English occupation (by now the English were no more safe in the interior of the island than had been the French two years before), and rumour was rife both in the fleet and in diplomatic circles that another weighty load was to be added to England's burden.

Spain, under the guidance of Godoy's helpless statesmanship, had already determined to yield to the influences which were acting upon Rome and Naples, and join France after deserting England. Her large but rotten fleet would be available for use against Jervis's squadron, and by her geographical position she would be able to interfere seriously with, if not to cut off altogether, the supply of that squadron. Jervis might at any moment find himself with neither base nor communications. Jervis was for holding on. He had begun, and had persevered with, the close blockade of Toulon, and he was confident that with the magnificent force under his hand he could defeat in detail the Spanish and French fleets should they attempt a junction. But the Cabinet was not in agreement. Orders came to Jervis to evacuate Corsica and retreat out of the Mediterranean.

Nelson was disappointed and hurt. While the English fleet kept its station off Toulon, Naples remained neutral and Corsica could be kept harmless—its ports would not be available for privateers. The communications of the Austrian army lay to a much greater extent across the Adriatic, from Trieste to Venice, than by the difficult route of the Brenner, and the retirement of the English would expose them to French attack. He guessed, with acute perception, that the Spaniards would enter the Mediterranean in force and expose themselves to a crushing defeat; and the event was to prove him right, although the English were not to be able to take advantage of the opportunity.

Corsica was in open revolt when Nelson, in obedience to Jervis's orders, arrived off Bastia, after an unavailing visit to Genoa to persuade that republic (menaced by overwhelming French forces) to continue, at least, neutral. He got Elliot and the troops safely away, although much material had to be abandoned, and, having undone the work which he himself had done most to achieve, he joined Jervis for the hoped-for battle. But Jervis had to retreat without fighting. Admiral Man had shown himself devoid of strategic genius. Backed by the opinion of a council of war (which 'did not fight'), he had gone to England from Gibraltar; and, in face of the superior numbers opposed to him, Jervis reluctantly sailed for Gibraltar, with his crews on one-third rations.

No sooner were they there than Nelson was sent back again. There were still English troops in Elba, and Jervis saw that it was his duty to bring them away. By his orders Nelson hoisted his broad pendant in the frigate *La Minerve*, and in company with the *Blanche*, started out on his perilous voyage. Five days later, off Cartagena, close on midnight, the two ships encountered two Spanish frigates, fought them ship to ship, and forced them to surrender. Nelson's prize proved to be the *Sabina*, commanded by Don Jacobo Stuart, a descendant of James II through the Duke of Berwick. *Sabina* had fought stoutly, and had suffered much damage, while *La Minerve* was also badly cut about. With a prize crew on board the *Sabina*, *La Minerve* pushed on with the former ship in tow, when suddenly out of the night emerged another Spanish frigate, which fired first into the prize and then engaged *La Minerve* in a hot fight for half an hour before she had had enough and wore away out of action. Pursuit was impossible, because with the dawn the whole Spanish fleet appeared, crowding on all sail towards the firing. Nelson fled, pursued by two ships of the line and two frigates, and, despite the damage done to *La Minerve*'s rigging, got clear away with the surprising good fortune which always helped him in his professional career—although his actual achievements are not to be attributed to it, save indirectly. The prize fell again into Spanish hands (the *Blanche*'s prize had already done so), but Nelson reached Porto Ferrajo without further incident.

Here he found the military commander unwilling to move. He had had no orders for evacuation, and he preferred, in consequence, to stay where he was, holding on to the island, in a position of most imminent peril—orders which he promptly obeyed were to reach him soon after. Nelson washed his hands of him; he got the naval stores on board, saw to it that transports and a small escort were ready to take the troops away when they decided to go, and he sent his convoy off as rapidly as possible. With Elliot and his staff on board as passengers—they were picked up at Naples— Nelson made the most of the easterly wind and hurried back. With his small frigates he ranged the length and breadth of the Western Mediterranean at a time when the French fleet commanded that sea unchallenged. He looked into San Fiorenzo, into Toulon and into Barcelona. The wind was foul for Port Mahon, so he omitted Minorca from his itinerary, but he looked into Cartagena, and at last, half frantic with impatience, he reached Gibraltar.

His deductions had been confirmed. The Spanish fleet had re-entered the Atlantic, and a battle was therefore imminent. Nelson was in a state of great anxiety lest he should miss the great opportunity of a fleet action under command of Jervis against superior numbers. It meant much to his career, and more still to his own personal feelings. His only delay at Gibraltar was to recover his prize crew by exchange, and then he dashed out again to find Jervis. In Gibraltar Bay lay two Spanish battleships and a frigate, who rushed after him in pursuit. They were overhauling him too, when a man fell overboard from *La Minerve*, and Lieutenant Hardy (the newly exchanged commander of the prize crew) was lowered in a boat to pick him up. The boat could not return without *La Minerve*'s way being checked. 'By God, I'll not lose Hardy! Back the mizzen topsail', said Nelson, in a fever. Hardy was picked up, and the pursuing ship of the line, astounded at the spectacle of the frigate backing topsails apparently to await action, hauled off until his consorts could arrive. Nelson had escaped once more.

Yet that self-same night *La Minerve* found strange ships all about her—she was in the midst of the Spanish fleet, and yet she got clear undetected, with the valuable information that the Spaniards were beating up towards Cadiz. Thirty-six hours later the English fleet was reached at its rendezvous, and the battle had not yet been fought. With a sigh of relief, Nelson went once more on board the *Captain*.

It was a fitting end of this first Mediterranean adventure. The cruise, which had begun with the capture of Toulon, had continued with voyages to Tunis and Naples, with actions with frigates and actions with fleets, innumerable fierce little actions on the Riviera coast, and the sieges of Bastia and Calvi, was now wound up by the complete circuit of the Western Mediterranean, a successful fight with an equal force of the enemy, three escapes from the enemy in overwhelming strength, and junction with the British fleet less than twenty-four hours before the most eventful naval battle since the Saints.

CHAPTER VIII

ST VINCENT AND SANTA CRUZ

AT dawn the next day the English fleet, running south-ward with the wind on the starboard beam, caught sight of the Spaniards standing across their course far ahead of them. Their twenty-seven ships of the line had straggled much during the night and had many of them fallen astern of station. Jervis had fifteen; allowance being made for three-deckers, the odds were three to two against him. But his fleet was well closed up, and he knew how capable were his Mediterranean-drilled units. 'England badly needs a victory at present', said Jervis, and plunged for the largest gap which presented itself in the Spanish line. The English fleet formed line ahead with beautiful precision, the *Captain* being third from the rear, and swept down to where the Spanish fleet was struggling unwieldily to concentrate. Wild signals had passed backwards and forwards between the main Spanish groups; there was a gap of eight miles between them, and the English were upon them before they could unite. Three only of the weather group succeeded in passing across the English van, raising the numbers of the lee group to nine. Troubridge in the *Culloden* was in a position to foil the others, who bore up to the northward. The lee division made an effort against the English line, but were beaten off by the crushing larboard broadsides of *Culloden*, *Blenheim*, and the rest. No ships in the world could beat to windward in the face of English gunfire. They held away again to the southward. Jervis had taken the opportunity offered him. His fifteen ships were close to eighteen Spaniards, and had cut off their retreat to leeward. It remained to be seen now whether the circumstances were such as to enable him to press the advantage. Round came his line in succession into the wind. Troubridge, in a fever of impatience, had long before made all ready for this signal to tack. Some say Jervis made it too late, but it seems as if, late though it was, earlier would have been too early. The English line was too short for the work it had to do. Be that as it may, the English line, tacking in succession, beat close-hauled northeastwards in pursuit of the eighteen Spaniards. The latter, in no sort of order, but inspired by a wild instinct of self-preservation, had bundled away northward and then turned away from the wind in an effort to pass across the English rear. Had the English line been five ships longer it would have been an impracticable manoeuvre; the Spaniards would have been caught between the English van and rear and destroyed. As it was they had a chance, some of them at least, of getting away to leeward of the English fleet by crossing their wake. The instant question arose, as to how to head them off. Nelson last but two in the line, decided to throw the *Captain* across their path.

For a hundred and more years the rigid line had been the fighting formation. For a captain to quit his station in the line was the most heinous crime known to the fighting instructions. Admiral Mathews had been broken by court-martial on that charge. Rodney had done it too; but his action had by no means met with universal approval. It was an unheard-of thing for a captain to do, but Nelson did it. He

gave the order to Captain Miller, and the *Captain* swung
round away from the wind, came up between the last two
ships in the English line and upon the five leading Spanish
ships—a four-decker, two three-deckers, an eighty and a
seventy-four. For a few minutes there was a furious inter-
change of fire, but the guns of the *Captain* worked with desperate rapidity, and succeeded in crippling the Spanish
leaders. The English van came up into action: Collingwood,
in the *Excellent*, the last ship in the line, had followed
Nelson's example after being ordered to do so by Jervis, and
came up to join in the mêlée. He blasted the *San Nicolas*,
with which *Captain* was engaged, with a crushing broadside
and dashed on after the Spanish flagship. The *San Nicolas*,
crippled, fell against the *San Josef*, and by Nelson's order the
Captain, disabled by that few minutes' concentrated fire,
came grinding up against the *San Nicolas*'s quarter.

Nelson called for boarders; Commander Berry, who was a
mere passenger, climbed on board from the spritsail yard. A
soldier serving as a marine broke a quarter gallery window,
and Nelson and the rest of the boarders rushed on board by
this route. They had to burst open the cabin doors to get out
to the spar deck, under fire from the skylights, but they succeeded, the Spanish-Irish commodore, Geraldino, being
killed. Dashing out on to the poop, Nelson found Berry
already there and the ship in his possession. But now the *San
Josef*, towering above the *San Nicolas*, opened a hot fire on the
latter's deck, killing friend and foe indiscriminately like the
Russians at Balaclava. Nelson's instant courage and energy
rose to the emergency. He called for reinforcements from the
Captain, and rushed on to the deck of the *San Josef*. The
Spaniards, thoroughly disconcerted, surrendered on the
spot, the Spanish captain announcing the news over the
quarter-deck rail, and Nelson, going up to the quarter-deck,

there received the swords of the Spanish officers, which one of his bargemen put under his arm, one after the other, as they were passed to him. Down below the Spanish-Dutch Rear-Admiral, Winthuysen, was dying of his wounds, while the lower-deck guns of the *San Nicolas* were still keeping up a hot fire on the *Prince George*, which had come up and was firing into her starboard bow. The firing soon ceased now that there was time for explanation, and the *Captain* lay a glorious wreck beside her two prizes while the rest of the fleet came up. Two others of the ships Nelson had checked were taken, but the *Santissima Trinidad* got away, after an unauthorized signal of surrender, thanks to the manner in which the *Excellent*'s rigging had been cut up.

Meanwhile the lee group of the Spaniards had at last worked round the English rear. There were at least twenty Spanish ships of the line in fighting order massed together now; Jervis had no more than twelve, thanks to the disablement of the ships of his van and rear. The odds were as heavily against him as ever, and his superhuman moment had passed. Jervis formed his fleet to cover his prizes and his cripples, and the two fleets gradually separated, the Spaniards standing for Cadiz, and the English for Lagos. It had been a well-timed and dramatic blow. The effect on the *moral* of the Spanish fleet and nation was most depressing. Cordova, the Spanish Admiral commanding, his surviving Rear-Admiral, and six Captains were court-martialled and dismissed from the Spanish service. The beaten fleet took refuge in Cadiz. Their progress had been checked just sufficiently for England, who was straining every nerve to increase her maritime forces, to reinforce Jervis to a strength which enabled him to resume the offensive attitude. In England the news arrived in time to counteract the depression caused by the evacuation of the Mediterranean, and to give national optimism a reserve to draw upon during the dark days of the approaching mutinies at Spithead and the Nore.

Jervis's terse official report on the day gave as much praise to Nelson as could be reasonably expected in such a marvel of compression, but from some of his colleagues Nelson received the most generous praise in private letters. He was given full credit in the service for his vigorous initiative, and since that day the tradition of the rigid fighting line has been modified to an extent which makes it hard for us now to realize the boldness of Nelson's action in departing from it; for that matter, there were isolated instances among Jervis's own subordinates of sharp criticism of his deeds. The influence of his example survived Nelson's death. Four generations later the battle orders of the Grand Fleet laid down the necessity for intelligent independent action by Captains and junior Admirals; in fact, the whole situation envisaged by those orders seems to cry out despairingly for a Nelson to arise and solve the hideously difficult problem presented. But at Jutland no Nelson arose: there was no one who could lay hold of the hesitant German fleet and delay its departure into the mist until the Grand Fleet could avenge the lost battlecruisers. Whether the circumstances allowed of any such manoeuvre is a matter of more doubt. Perhaps even Nelson, had he held a subordinate command at Jutland, might have believed any unrehearsed manoeuvre impracticable, and would have been content to continue with the lumbering deployment which left the Germans unheld and unbeaten. But one doubts it even while one has not the presumption nor the ability to make suggestions.

Immediately after St Vincent had been fought Nelson had become a Rear-Admiral, although news of the promotion had not yet reached him. He was made Rear-Admiral because he

had been Captain; similarly, he was made a Knight of the
Bath, not as the man who broke from the line and headed off
the Spaniards, but as a Commodore junior to the Admiral
who had won a battle. These things were a matter of precedent. Jervis received an earldom and became Lord St
Vincent—one of the earliest English titles to be derived
from a foreign place, to be paralleled with the Earldom of
Ypres and the Marquisate of Douro—while Nelson's portion
would have been a baronetcy had he not used his influence
with Elliot to beg for the ribbon and star instead.
Subsequently he was to receive a bill for £400 from the her-
alds for their services, which he was indignantly to refuse to
pay, following a precedent which was later to be invoked by,
amongst others, Lords Roberts and Kitchener. He had more
than one motive in asking for the Bath. In the first place, he
pictured himself in retirement with his wife, and imagined
that Sir Horatio Nelson, KB, could live in a cottage and be
less out of place than Sir Horatio Nelson, Bt. In the second
place, it was his opinion that the Order was a surer hall-mark
of distinction. People could be more certain that a Knight of
the Bath had done something worth doing than they could
with a baronet, and it was certainly true that at this period
the reorganized Order was a definite reward of merit in a way
peerages and Garters were not. Then there can be little
doubt that Nelson liked having an Order to wear; he was
proud of his 'chains and medals' and bright toys, and indeed
he had the stars of his Orders embroidered on his coat.
There may be another and more obscure motive for the
preference too, which will be discussed in a later chapter.

The English fleet had refitted with the celerity to be
expected of the magnificent seamen who manned it.
Portugal's friendship meant much to a fleet engaged in the
blockade of Cadiz, and the Tagus was a far more convenient

base for the purpose than was Gibraltar. From Lisbon Nelson sailed in the *Irresistible* with two more ships of the line in an endeavour to intercept the treasure ships which were on their way to Spain with the gold of the Americas. It was a coveted and eminently desirable mission; every one in the navy recalled with longing the occasion when the *Active* and the *Favourite* captured the Lima treasure ship off Cadiz in 1762, so full of gold that the captains received £65,000 each and every seaman £484. Success would give Nelson the wealth of which his continual generosity kept him in need, but during the cruise he was repeatedly writing suggestions to Jervis which would take him away from this profitable possibility. His main source of anxiety was the safety of the English garrison of Elba, which had declined his convoy before St Vincent. It comprised over three thousand troops in all, and to England the loss of three thousand troops would in those days be a terrible blow. At the time of writing it was about to sail for England from Elba with only a frigate escort, and there was more than a slight chance that on the way to Gibraltar it might encounter French ships of the line from Toulon and experience a terrible disaster. Nelson's pleadings with Lord St Vincent (as Sir John Jervis had become) ended in the latter's yielding and taking the risk that the Spaniards might emerge from Cadiz and find him without all his forces concentrated. Nelson with the *Captain* and another ship of the line was sent up the Mediterranean to meet the transports. They narrowly avoided a French squadron of overwhelming strength and brought the whole convoy safely to Gibraltar.

St Vincent's fears regarding a sally by the Spanish fleet proved baseless. On the contrary, the whole energies of the blockading squadron were now devoted to finding a solution of the time-honoured problem of how to force the blockaded

fleet to come out. The active part of the business was
entrusted to Nelson. Despite the presence in the fleet of
two junior Admirals senior to him, he was given the command of the inshore squadron, augmented to ten sail of the
line out of twenty, and of the boats of the fleet and the gun-
boat flotilla. The main objective was to bring the gunboats
into range of the Spanish ships in the long harbour of
Cadiz—a matter of enormous difficulty, in view of the batteries which the Spaniards hurriedly mounted and the activity of their flotilla. Three different night attacks were
launched with no great result. For the first two only one
bomb vessel was available, and she was hit at last so severely
by the shore batteries that she had to be withdrawn, but in
each case there was some desperate boat fighting. In the second attack Nelson in his barge with Captain Freemantle and
eleven men fought to a finish with the Spanish flotilla
commander with four officers and twenty-six men in a large
launch. All the Spaniards were killed or wounded, and the
launch was captured. Nelson later said that it was on this
occasion that his personal courage was most conspicuous;
and it was during the fray that John Sykes saved Nelson's life
by interposing his own head to receive a sabre cut aimed at
Nelson.

All that the desperate courage displayed by the attackers
achieved was to force the Spanish fleet into the inner harbour, so that the English would have longer notice of a sortie, although Nelson declared in private letters that had his
orders been obeyed in the last attack the whole Spanish
flotilla would have been taken. Everybody knows how difficult it is to carry out orders exactly in a night attack, and this
one was launched in an involved harbour with reliance
placed, perforce, on a treacherous wind.

All this activity on the part of the English was very

necessary. At the time the fleet at Spithead was in open mutiny (although the term seems a drastic description of the very orderly behaviour of the seamen), and more than one of St Vincent's ships had the same infection. Nelson's own flagship, the *Theseus*, newly arrived from Portsmouth, was for a time gravely affected, until Nelson's personality won the men over. After all, the men had much to complain of, being largely forced into a service whose pay had not been raised from the time of Charles II, and fed upon provisions so bad and scanty that, as Admiral Raigersfeld tells us, rats caught on board ship had a ready sale as dainties even among the officers. The subsequent mutiny at the Nore, after the men's demands had largely been satisfied, had more of a political aim, and it seems as if a plot with the same ends was hatching in St Vincent's fleet. Activity to keep the men's minds occupied was very necessary; moreover, some severe examples had to be made, and St Vincent was the man to make them. The executions he ordered had Nelson's complete approval—the senior Vice-Admiral, Thompson, actually had the effrontery to protest, publicly and in writing against their being carried into effect on a Sunday, whereupon he was very properly sent home on the spot by his iron-handed Commander-in-Chief. Yet it is well worth noting that during this period Nelson did all he could, and successfully, to prevent the execution of other mutineers whom he was convinced were insane.

Meanwhile news had arrived that the Manila treasure ship had taken refuge at Tenerife in the Canaries, where already lay the Viceroy of Mexico, with the wealth for which Nelson had earlier been on the watch. The prize was tempting. Some time before, St Vincent, at Nelson's suggestion, had tried to induce the commander of the Elba garrison to depart from his orders and join the fleet in an assault upon Tenerife;

the three thousand British infantry which comprised his
command, with the siege equipment at their disposal, would
probably have made short work of the slender Spanish garrison. However, General de Burgh had declined the invitation—his earlier behaviour with regard to the evacuation of
Elba had shown his meticulous sense of obedience to
orders—and it seems likely that his refusal was approved at
home. A state of affairs in which a sixth of the available
British expeditionary force went off on its own initiative on
extemporized attacks on outlying enemy possessions would
be intolerable and dangerous, as likely to lead to unforeseen
entanglements and commitments.

So if the attempt were to be made, it must be done by St
Vincent's fleet alone. The Admiral himself was not very hopeful, but Nelson, who appreciated the magnitude of the prize
and the smallness of the stake (and, perhaps, being rather
uplifted by four years of continued good fortune), was pressing, and at last St Vincent gave way and issued orders to
Nelson to take three ships of the line, four frigates, and a cut-
ter, to proceed with them to Tenerife, and there to take possession of the treasure on the island or alternatively to raise a
contribution on the inhabitants. Nelson was given additional
marines and ratings for a landing party; altogether the
squadron had a thousand men available for this purpose, and
Troubridge of the *Culloden* was designated to command them.

The original plan had been to land this party from the
frigates at night, while the ships of the line kept below the
horizon to convince the garrison that it was only a reconnoitring force approaching the island, but the design failed
because wind and current kept the frigates too far from shore
during the hours of darkness. Next morning Troubridge
became convinced that, if he could only establish his force
on the heights above the fort he had hoped to surprise, he

could frighten it into surrender. Despite his conviction, he refrained from acting upon it until Nelson had arrived and had given permission for the attempt, and by that time— several hours after dawn—the inhabitants had recovered from the surprise and had occupied the heights with a considerable army. A naval landing force was much too valuable to be risked in a forlorn assault on such a position. The wind died away and the currents prevented the ships of the line from working into range of the fort, and by the evening failure was admitted and the landing party called off. Whether Troubridge was right or not in his belief that the occupation of the heights would ensure the fall of the fort it is impossible to say; Nelson thought he was, and was vexed that Troubridge had not acted on his own responsibility. The moral effect of surprise would have been great, and the appearance of a landing force a thousand strong from four frigates must certainly have been unexpected. It is not hard to guess what Nelson would have done had he been in Troubridge's position.

There was now no possibility of surprise, and most men might have abandoned the whole project. For the defence of Santa Cruz there were some eight thousand men available, many of them regular infantry, and there was a strong citadel to be taken before victory was probable. A direct assault seemed hopeless now that the island had been thoroughly warned. But perhaps it would be so unlooked for as to command success by its very unexpectedness. There was a slight chance of a bold stroke succeeding, and no one knew for certain if the Spanish troops would stand and fight—what Nelson had seen of them at Toulon had led him to expect the contrary; he had not at his disposal the experience of the Peninsular War, which went to show that it was the cream of the Spanish army which was employed in the outlying garrisons.

A tiresome beat to windward for thirty hours was necessary before Nelson had all his force in the immediate vicinity of Santa Cruz, and orders were issued for an assault from
boats upon the town that night. Nelson was going to take the
risk; he realized the danger and the chances against success,
but his belief was that the *moral* of the personnel and the
national prestige would be more depressed by a tame with-
drawal than by the repulse of a bold attack. He himself went
into action with the presentiment of death upon him.

The attack was launched at eleven o'clock at night, the
boats moving off, crammed with men, into the darkness,
with a heavy sea running and a raging surf breaking on the
beach. Their advance was observed, fire opened, bells rang,
and the garrison was ready. Nelson's orders had been for a
massed attack on the mole, but only a few boats besides his
own could find it in the darkness. With his handful of men
he landed in face of terrific fire of grape and musketry. He
himself fell at the moment of landing, his right elbow broken
by a grapeshot. Those with him fought their way to the end
of the mole, and captured the guns there, but were driven
back by fire from the citadel. They gave up the hopeless
attempt, and with their wounded leader the very few survivors pushed back across a raging sea to the ships. The cut-
ter *Fox* had been hard hit by the batteries, and sank suddenly
at that moment with a hundred men on board, and Nelson,
tossing in that tiny boat, with Nisbet, his stepson, struggling
to bind up his shattered arm, insisted on helping to save
some of the wretched men in the water. They reached the
Seahorse, but Nelson would not go on board of her, because
Mrs Freemantle was there and he would not shock her with
his appearance. At last they came to the *Theseus*, and then, by
the doubtful light of swaying lanterns, the shattered arm was
amputated.

Meanwhile the rest of the force had struggled to shore through a raging surf which stove the boats, wetted the ammunition, and lost for them the scaling ladders and other material for the assault. Troubridge gathered a few men together and fought his way through to the rendezvous, but daylight revealed every approach to the citadel guarded by thousands of men. His boats were stove, he had no provisions and little ammunition, but with marvellous audacity (quite different from his behaviour four days before) he coolly threatened to burn the town unless he was allowed to depart and provided with boats to embark. The amazed Spaniards granted him these terms on the spot, and what threatened to be a very serious disaster was minimized into a mere repulse.

CHAPTER IX

THE NILE

THERE followed a weary, depressing, three-weeks-long journey back to Cadiz. Nelson was utterly depressed. He reproached himself for the failure at Tenerife, certain that if he had assumed the command of the first landing party he would have been successful. The loss of his arm convinced him that he would no longer be employed at sea— it would constitute a very serious handicap when going on board or disembarking from a ship in bad weather—and his wound gave him very considerable pain. The silk ligature which had been applied to the brachial artery could not be absorbed as would one of the usual material of gut, and it would continue to hurt him until it sloughed away; and Nelson, with unusual irritation, refused to have the stump treated while on the way to Cadiz, with the result that the closing of the wound and the shortness of the stump rendered any further interference inadvisable.

St Vincent's reception of him, however, did something to ease his depression. The grim old Admiral wrote that Nelson had done all there was to be done, had succeeded beyond expectation, and had nothing about which to reproach himself. He allowed himself to be influenced by Nelson's request for promotion for Josiah Nisbet, and made that young man Commander at the age of seventeen—the first important step in a career which was to lead to an early captaincy, alcoholism and insanity. Nelson he sent home; ten days later he arrived at Portsmouth, after three and a half years of continuous service, during which he had been engaged in twenty-three actions at sea and in four months' active service on land.

His wife was not at Portsmouth to welcome him on that September day. She could not, of course, be sure of the date of his arrival, and she was occupied at Bath with attendance on Nelson's father. She knew already of his wound; he had written to her with his left hand while on his way to Cadiz—one of his odd brotherly letters, beginning 'My dearest Fanny' and ending 'believe me, your affectionate husband', with never an endearment throughout its length (except 'I shall feel rich if I enjoy your affection') and every word bridled with the extraordinary restraint he always used in his letters to her. But he joined her at Bath—we know no details of their meeting—and began a long convalescence. Lady Nelson learnt how to dress his wound, which caused him increasing agony until the ligature came away in December. So acute was the pain that more than once opium had to be employed to give him relief.

His recovery was not too tardy, all the same. His reception in England was even more flattering than had been his reception by St Vincent. He received charming and sympathetic letters from all his correspondents whose good opinion was welcome or useful—Lord Spencer, the Duke of Clarence, Lord Hood. The King received him at his investiture with marked personal attention. A pension—nominally £1000 a year, actually only £700—was awarded him, although he had written to his wife that he expected to be left 'in want of pecuniary assistance', while two years' pay as wound gratuities was a very decided help towards relief from his continual shortage of money. The most effective agency towards his cure, however, was the discovery that he was not to be (as he had expressed it to St Vincent) 'a burden to his friends and useless to his country'. The country was to find use for 'a left-handed admiral'. He was not to be left to languish in his 'very humble cottage'. Authority was aware of his talents, and was anxious to employ them as soon as he was well. There was work for him. Nelson was hardly likely to remain ill a day longer than would suffice for his bare recovery with that prospect before him.

The first suggestion was to give him the *Foudroyant*, a vessel not yet completed, but the best designed ship in the navy. But he seemed likely to be fit for service before she was launched, and another had to be found. He had already chosen his Flag Captain—Berry, a lucky man. He had chanced, as a newly promoted Commander, to be on the *Captain* as an additional officer on the day of St Vincent, and had been promoted again by Jervis for his gallantry in leading the boarders. He was a young man in consequence; he had fallen under the spell of Nelson's personality, and Nelson had conceived for him the affection he was always ready to bestow upon young men—which he had given to young Andrews, his former sweetheart's brother; to Josiah Nisbet; and was to give to young Parker. The result in this case was to give Berry a most important command as his first appointment; he was to be Sir Edward Berry within the year, and a man of mark and achievement.

On the 4th December the ligature came away from the artery; on December 8th Nelson sent to the parish church of St George's a request—'an officer wishes to return thanks to Almighty God for his perfect recovery from a severe wound'—on the 14th March he took leave of the King, and on the 29th he hoisted his flag on the *Vanguard* at Spithead.

Theseus Augt 16th: 1797,

My Dear Sir,

I rejoice at being once more in sight of your flag, and with your permission will come on board the Ville de Paris & pay you my respects. If the Emerald has joined, you know my wishes, a left handed Admiral will never again be considered as useful therefore the sooner I get to a very humble cottage the better and make room for a better man to serve the State but whatever be my lot believe me with the most sincere affection for your most faithful

Turn over   *Horatio Nelson*

A facsimile of one of Nelson's first left-handed letters after he had lost his arm as a result of being shot at Tenerife in July 1797, written to Lord St Vincent, and which contains that universal sentiment of seamen throughout the ages – to retire to the peace and quiet of a country cottage. It reads:

Theseus August 16th 1797

'My Dear Sir,
I rejoice at being once more in sight of your flag, and with your permission will come on board the Ville de Paris, and pay you my respects. If the Emerald has joined you know my wishes. A left-handed admiral will never again be considered as useful, therefore the sooner I get to a very humble cottage the better, and make way for a better man to serve the State; but whatever be my lot, believe me, with most sincere affection, ever your most faithful,

Horatio Nelson'

A pencil sketch of Nelson drawn by Simon De Koster. It was, apparently, done for
Lady Hamilton herself, at Merton, a few days before Nelson sailed for Copenhagen.
It is of particular interest as it was the portrait that Nelson believed to be most like
him.

An engraving of the Old Parsonage at Burnham Thorpe, Norfolk, Nelson's birthplace. Tradition holds that the figure in the foreground is Nelson's father, Edmund. The Parsonage was demolished in 1803.

Nelson's wife Frances – 'Fanny' – portrayed by Henry Edridge when she was about forty.

Emma as 'Nature', 1782, a portrait commissioned by Charles Greville. This was the first portrait for which Emma sat for the artist George Romney.

The destruction of the French ship *L'Orient* at the battle of the Nile, 1 August 1798, painted by Mather Brown. This was Nelson's first great victory and dealt a fatal blow to Bonaparte's ambitions in the Middle East.

A Nile memorial, erected by Captain Charles Herbert, Earl Manvers, at Thoresby Hall in Nottinghamshire. Nelson's heroic status, confirmed after the battle of the Nile, spawned monuments, both private and public, throughout Britain, Ireland, the Americas and Canada.

(Top) *Dido in Despair* by Gillray, 1801. As Nelson's fleet sails to sea Emma laments 'Ah where, and ah where is my gallant Sailor gone?' Nelson's affair with Emma was a very public one, and a national hero, falling for the understandable temptations of the flesh, became an inevitable target of the satirists of the day.

(Above) An oblique drawing of the battle of Trafalgar, by Nicholas Pocock, depicting the approach to battle. *Victory* leads the port-hand, windward, column towards the centre of the French and Spanish line which has sagged to loo'ard in the light airs.

(Top) *The Death of Nelson* by Arthur William Devis, 1807. Devis spent three weeks on board *Victory*, after her return to England with Nelson's body, where he sketched the ship's company and attended the autopsy carried out by Dr Beatty. The latter experience surely influenced the livid nature of face and body.

(Above) *Victory*, carrying Nelson's body, is depicted running up Channel by J M W Turner. The body was transferred to the *Chatham* at the Nore and then taken to Greenwich where it lay in state. Nelson was finally buried in St Paul's on 9 January 1806, after 'one of the most splendid solemnities that ever took place in this country'.

The greatest memorial of all. HMS *Victory*, still a fully-commissioned ship in the Royal Navy, flies the signal 'Every man shall do his duty' each year on Trafalgar Day.

It had been a very quiet seven months that he had spent in England; most of his leave had been passed at Bath, although he and Lady Nelson had spent a good deal of time in lodgings at 141 Bond St. His domestic happiness had been complete—or at least as complete as he thought domestic happiness could be—and amid the general chorus of approval of his achievements there had been only one dissentient voice, that of Vice-Admiral William Parker, whose flag had been flying in the third ship of the English line, the *Prince George*, at St Vincent. Parker took violent exception to the exultant account of the battle which Nelson prepared for the press, especially to the statement that for nearly an hour the *Captain* and the *Culloden* had borne the Spanish fleet unsupported. Parker pointed out that this could only have been the case if the *Prince George* had held back, and Nelson, with a curtness which may have implied sincerity but was not at all tactful, promptly agreed without reducing his estimate of the time. Parker tried to maintain a controversy, but he had little command of English or of influence, and the matter dropped by the time Nelson left England again.

By the time Nelson sailed from Spithead England had been left quite without allies in her struggle with France. Austria, beaten into helplessness by the continuous punishment administered in Italy by Bonaparte, had made the peace France wanted; the Austrian Netherlands were ceded to France, French influence was acknowledged in Piedmont and the Milanese, the French frontier was advanced to the Rhine, and as compensation Austria was admitted an accomplice in the spoliation of the old order by the gift of Venetia. The international situation was now that of the time of the American War of Independence; England was at war with France, the Netherlands and Spain, and was without a powerful Continental ally to keep France busy and wear down her resources. Yet the moment was not so fraught with immediate danger; Duncan at Camperdown had destroyed the Dutch fleet; the First of June, the capture of Toulon, the Mediterranean fighting, the battle off Brest, prolonged blockade, and the Revolution had between them all weakened French naval strength. St Vincent and Godoy's administration had ruined the Spanish fleet. England had had five years in which to recover from Pitt's economics, and those five years of naval war had raised her navy to a lofty pitch of professional efficiency. The balance of naval power in the last war had inclined slightly against England; in this war it was even now decidedly in England's favour, and it remained to be seen what use England would make of her advantage. She was building ships as fast as she could man them; Camperdown had relieved her of much of the strain on her present resources; to St Vincent off Cadiz lavish promises were made of approaching reinforcements, and as earnest of them Nelson arrived in the *Vanguard*. St Vincent wrote that his arrival had given him new life—and St Vincent was no dealer in hyperbole—and two days after Nelson reached Cadiz, St Vincent was already addressing 'most secret' orders to him regarding a new mission, one of so much responsibility and difficulty that he had not dared to entrust it to any of his other flag-officers.

The French and the French–Italian coast was, and had been for some time, alive with preparations. Ships of the line were refitting in numbers at Toulon; hundreds of transports were being made ready in every port from Marseilles to Leghorn; the Swiss confederacy had been plundered to provide money; thousands of troops lay in readiness on the coast. Some tremendous stroke was being meditated; but what it was could not be ascertained. France could employ troops with effect (once she could get them there) in the

West Indies, in Ireland (this was the year '98), in Italy. Not
merely that, but such was the state of her declared national
doctrine that all governments could be considered her enemies if it suited her; she could strike at an unoffending neutral if she wished, and no Frenchman in France would
protest. Any point in the whole world therefore might be the
objective of this armament. The mobilization of troops, too,
might easily be a mere feint. France could afford it. The
design might merely be a union with the Spanish fleets at
Cadiz or Cartagena or with the French at Brest. The enormous uncertainty had harassed St Vincent for some weeks
now, and it was a relief to have at his disposal Nelson's services to clear up the mystery and to guard against surprise.

On May 2nd Nelson had his orders. He was to take the
Vanguard, *Orion* and *Alexander* with four frigates into the
Mediterranean. He was to gather information about the new
French armament, and about the Cartagena squadron; if the
French came out he was to find whither they were bound, and
if they passed the Straits of Gibraltar he was to pass them
first, so that St Vincent would have his force concentrated
and between the French and the Spaniards. It was a dangerous as well as a difficult task to entrust to such a small
squadron, but St Vincent could spare him no greater one until
the arrival of the promised reinforcements from England.
Nelson, however, took over the command with no misgivings
whatever; his letter to his wife, in its usual cautious strain,
tells her that he has found the Cadiz squadron too well pro-
tected to be vulnerable, and that he is being detached by St
Vincent, but 'not on any fighting expedition'. Nelson, even
when writing to his wife, kept strictly to the duty of silence
imposed by the 'most secret' heading of his orders.

He left Gibraltar on May 8th, pushed up into the Lion
Gulf, gathered a few scraps of information, and on the 20th

met with a tremendous gale, in which the *Vanguard* rolled her
foremast and her main and mizzen topmasts overboard—
accidents which rather hint that Captain Berry had not been
as attentive to the well-being of his ship as he might have
been, or as an older man might have been. The frigates were
separated in the gale, but Captain Ball in the *Alexander* came
to the rescue and took the *Vanguard* in tow. For several hours
the two ships were in desperate danger, and Nelson once
actually ordered Ball to cast off and save himself, but Ball
hung on, and by staunch good seamanship worked both
vessels out of the danger in which they lay of being cast on
the Sardinian coast into the shelter of the San Pietro Islands,
south of Sardinia. There, under faint protest from the
Sardinian Government, the united efforts of every man in
the ships re-rigged the *Vanguard* with jury masts in four days.
The *Vanguard* was a fast sailer—trust Nelson to choose one
such—and the jury rig fortunately did not reduce her speed
below what was desirable in a ship of the line. The catastrophe was entirely repaired therefore without having to
return to port.

At once Nelson set sail for the rendezvous he had
appointed for the squadron in case of separation. The very
next day they fell in with a vessel from Marseilles, from
which they got the information that Bonaparte had sailed,
with thirteen ships of the line, four hundred transports, and
thirty thousand troops, the day before the great gale which
had dismasted the *Vanguard*. In a fury of excitement Nelson
pushed on to the rendezvous. He reached it on June 4th—
and the frigates were not there! But next morning came
Hardy in the *Mutine* brig bearing good news and bad. The
frigates were gone beyond recall—their senior captain had
seen *Vanguard*'s masts go before the separation, and on his
own responsibility had sailed for Gibraltar, certain that such

damage would send Nelson there too. But to make up for
that a powerful squadron of ships of the line were on their
way to him.

Lord Spencer in London had sent reinforcements and
fresh orders to St Vincent. The English flag was to be displayed in strength in the Mediterranean as an important
political factor in the formation of a new coalition and to
baulk the rumoured French armament around Toulon. If St
Vincent did not see fit to go himself, he must send a strong
detachment, and in that case Lord Spencer most earnestly
recommended that the detachment be placed under the
command of Sir H Nelson, 'whose acquaintance with that
part of the world, as well as his activity and disposition, seem
to qualify him in a peculiar manner for that service'. Nelson
was to have his chance, the one so longed for by every officer
in the service, and attained by so few, to command an English
fleet against the enemy. So far his reputation was built up on
his record of dash and activity and independence of thought;
perhaps his best-known achievement up till now was not his
epoch-making leaving of the line at St Vincent, but his boarding of the *San Josef*, across the decks of the captured *San
Nicolas*, a feat which might be expected of any fighting routine officer. Now he was to be given an immense problem to
solve, one involving ocean-wide strategy and immense political consequences, and the successful solution of that problem
would bring about the immediate presentation of another,
more ordinary problem—of winning the battle this success
made possible. Thirteen ships of the line were to constitute
his command—a large force, enormous, indeed, for the command of a very junior Rear-Admiral. There are few parallels
for such a responsibility being given to a man so low on the
list, and perhaps the best one is the appointment of Admiral
Beatty to the Battle Cruiser Squadron in 1913—at much the

same age as Nelson at this time and after holding Admiral's
rank for about the same time. Yet while the compliment was
great, the responsibility was correspondingly enormous; in
England there was a very sensitive public and an envenomed
Opposition who would condemn any mistake unhesitatingly.
There was no censorship like that which, in 1914, was to per-
mit the public to regard the escape of the *Goeben* to
Constantinople as a British victory.

There is very much of a likeness, indeed, between the
problem presented to Nelson in June 1798, and that presented to Sir Berkeley Milne in July and August, 1914. In
each case there was no obvious objective for the hostile
force; Admiral Souchon had just as few open friends as
General Bonaparte had open enemies. It was as unthinkable
that *Goeben* should be welcomed by neutral Turkey as that
Bonaparte should fling himself and his thirty thousand men
upon a province of the same unoffending power. The apparent probability that Souchon would make for the Adriatic is
balanced by the apparent probability that Bonaparte would
make for Sicily. Sir Berkeley Milne was indeed further handi-
capped by the fact that Souchon himself did not at first
know where he was going, and really purposeless movements
should be more confusing than studied feints, while the
British Government's tenderness for Italian neutrality in
1914 finds no real counterpart in the orders to Nelson, but
Nelson was troubled by a lack of the scouting vessels with
which Milne was well supplied.

The Admiralty's orders to St Vincent, and his to Nelson,
offered an astonishing array of possibilities to their selection
as to where this thirty thousand men, thirteen ships of the
line, and four hundred transports were likely to go. The
enormous force was borne on the Mediterranean, lost to
sight; it was like having a man with homicidal tendencies

and well armed at liberty in a crowded room full of furniture in pitch darkness. St Vincent's orders to Nelson envisaged primarily attacks upon Naples or Sicily, a conveyance of the troops to Spain (for the purpose of action against Portugal) or a dash through the Straits against Ireland. A subsequent paragraph added to these divergent possibilities 'any part of the Mediterranean', together with the Morea, the Greek islands, the Adriatic and, for the matter of that, the Black Sea. Nelson's business was to make the right choice out of this mass, with only his native wits to help him, aided by what he knew of weather conditions in the Mediterranean and by any casual scraps of information he might pick up *after* setting his course in what might be the wrong direction.

Whatever he might decide to do, there was no time to be lost. Feverishly Nelson spread out his three ships to make sure of meeting the reinforcement. It was his own *Vanguard* which encountered it—ten ships of the line under the command of Troubridge. Nelson's large squadron was not to be burdened with other Admirals and potential seconds in command, although it was large enough to justify the presence of at least one, if not two. There were, in fact, very few Admirals junior to Nelson, and none of them was with St Vincent, so that if Nelson were to command he must be the only flag-officer present. Any detachment he might make—and it might be a large one—must be entrusted to a Captain. It seems as if Nelson wrung an advantage even out of this circumstance where no advantage can be clearly seen.

Orion and *Alexander* were not in sight when Troubridge joined, but Nelson neither dared nor wished to await their return. With his eleven ships of the line he dashed off, leaving his sole frigate on the rendezvous to re-direct them. He swept off round the north of Corsica and down the Italian coast, questing widely in his initial cast. *Orion* and *Alexander* rejoined. Uncertain information came in that the French had been seen off Sicily on an eastward course. Nelson had already put his finger on the exact point of Bonaparte's aim in an early letter to Lord Spencer, wherein he announced his conviction that if the French passed Sicily they would go on to Alexandria. The fleet reached Naples. Troubridge had been sent on earlier in the *Mutine* in quest of information. He came back to where the fleet lay hove-to outside neutral waters with the news that the French had last been seen about to attack Malta. The other information he brought regarding the decision of the Neapolitan Government to maintain at least a form of neutrality was not at the moment of such burning importance, but it inspired Nelson to write a clear and caustic letter to Hamilton pointing out the immense advantages a declaration of war against France would bring to Naples—advantages which Nelson saw clearly enough while he was hankering after the loan of Neapolitan frigates to replace his lost English ones, and of gunboats and bomb vessels should the French be sheltering in Valetta, but which were not to be too apparent in the following year nor in 1806.

Malta, then, was the point to aim at, and so off they went through the Straits of Messina; but on June 22nd came information—from a doubtful source, but circumstantial enough—that Malta had fallen on the 15th to the French, who had sailed again next day. This last was incorrect; the French did not sail until the 19th, but Nelson had to act on the information. He could not spend time beating against the westerly wind which was still blowing, with the chance that on his arrival at Malta he might have to beat back against an easterly one. There was no news of a landing in Sicily, which he would surely have got had one taken place.

Alexandria next, then, as he had already decided. To Alexandria with a fair wind took the fleet six days, six days of pressing anxiety and absence of news, for the few ships spoken had none to give. Yet at Alexandria when they reached it there was no sign of the French. The authorities on land, and the British consul in the town, had not even heard of any possibility of an attack. There was dismay among the captains, who knew the terrible responsibility which rested upon Nelson's shoulders; but Nelson bore the blow unflinching, although with annoyance. The likeliest possibility had not eventuated: they must proceed now with the less likely, as speedily as they might. With the six days' start Nelson believed the French to have he could not have passed them on the way. Without an instant's delay the fleet rushed on, to the Aleppo coast, and westward past Crete to complete the round back to Sicily. In the thousands of miles travelled there came no news, no whisper, about the French fleet. For four weeks there had been none, by now.

Nelson could not know that the Sicilian information was false, nor that the night after his departure from Sicily he had passed at night and in thick weather, close beside the huge French convoy without seeing a sign of them. If he had found them the world might, probably would, have witnessed a more colossal disaster on the sea than the defeat of the Armada. Nelson's plans were made. Two-thirds of his fleet was to have kept the French ships of the line occupied while the other third dashed in amongst the helpless transports. The English would have been hard hit, beaten perhaps, but the French losses must have been monstrous. The English seamanship was too good for the French to be able to foil their plan; the crowded transports must have been sunk or burned in dozens, for a sailing fleet cannot scatter to the four quarters of the compass.

But, as it was, here was Nelson back in Syracuse, worn out with anxiety, hindered and hampered by the determination of the Sicilian Court not to bring down the wrath of France upon themselves by a too liberal stretching of the rules of neutrality, pursuing St Vincent's despatches from Cape Passaro to Naples and back again to Cape Passaro; still without a word of the French, but with information that St Vincent's two other Admirals, Parker and Orde, had protested so violently against Nelson's being given the command of the Mediterranean detachment that he was sending them home—where they would be two venomous and influential enemies who would head the outcry against any mistake Nelson had made.

The difficulties raised by the Neapolitan Government were overcome in five days, whether or not (as has been hotly debated) Lady Hamilton had anything to do with it. Nelson was, indeed, empowered and prepared to exact assistance from Sicily by force, and he expected the Neapolitan Court to yield with public protest while sending private orders to the local authority to be as helpful as possible. Nelson believed at that time (although he changed his mind later) that no such private order was given. Nevertheless, as has been said, the necessities of the squadron were met without great delay (any delay would seem monstrous to Nelson searching for an enemy), and on the 25th July they were off again. Whither could they go this time? The French were certainly not to the westward of Italy; the absence of news and the past weather conditions guaranteed that. It could only be the Morea and Constantinople, now that Syria and Egypt were ruled out. To the Morea they went, and there, after a quick passage, they found not the French, but news that a whole month earlier the French had been seen from Crete on a south-easterly course. Round came the ships

again, once more on a course for Egypt, and then at last, on
the afternoon of August 1st, a signal from the *Zealous*
announced that the long chase, of nearly eight weeks' dura-
tion, had ended in the overtaking of the quarry. The French
ships of war were at anchor in the Bay of Aboukir.

During those eight weeks Nelson had developed a
system which had raised the fighting value of his squadron
enormously. Not content with the routine exercises in
gunnery, he had formed a habit of summoning his Captains
in ones and twos and batches on board his flagship and working out with them in conversation the methods of attack on
the French fleet when they encountered it. It was an inno-
vation to a great extent—one cannot picture Rodney or
Jervis doing the same—and it was successful. It confirmed
and remoulded the tradition of naval brotherhood, which had
become sadly weakened during the bad times of the Seven
Years' War and the War of American Independence. It did
away with the necessity for a formal line of battle which had
been imposed partly by fear that with a freer hand a Captain
might take advantage of this latitude and leave his fellows in
the lurch, either through cowardice or personal dislike; it
must be remembered that at Camperdown, only the year
before, more than one Captain had misbehaved. Where
every Captain was a personal friend of all the others and
further devoted to his Admiral, there was no fear of similar
incidents; the only fear now was lest hot-headed emulation
might lead to a plunge into battle under disadvantageous
conditions. This, on the other hand, was prevented by the
long discussions on board the *Vanguard*. Nelson's Captains,
young men and middle-aged, fiery and cautious, thoughtful
and heedless, had, under the presidency of their
Commander, worked out possibilities of every kind, each
contributing to the general fund his experience or

knowledge of naval battles fought in every quarter of the globe. The principle, so simple to express and so difficult to attain, of bringing superior force upon the vital point, had been insisted upon and debated until every Captain knew what he was expected to do to bring it about, and could be relied upon to carry out his part both with goodwill and of course with the seamanship necessary. But the credit is Nelson's actually as well as technically. A quarrelsome or fault-finding Admiral, a Bligh or a Byng, could never have dared to entrust his reputation to his Captains as Nelson did, leaving out of consideration the question as to whether these men had the ingenuity to devise a plan to bring more guns into effective action than the enemy.

The French fleet was anchored on the edge of shoal water, with the island of Aboukir to the windward end of the line. Brueys, the French Admiral, had not made the most of his position: there was room for the English to pass round the head of the line between it and the island, there was room for the English to pass between the line and the shore, and there was room for ships to pass through the intervals of the line. Apparently, however, his estimate of the potentialities of seamanship was low enough for him to be able to leave these possibilities out of account—as he might perhaps have done had he been expecting attack by a French fleet. He had apparently thought that the only routes open for attack were from seaward and from to-leeward, and it was at the seaward curve of his line, his centre, that he had placed his most powerful ships. In the course of his three weeks' stay (according to Napoleon's unreliable testimony this stay was against Napoleon's wishes) he had done surprisingly little towards establishing batteries on Aboukir Island. In general, his dispositions were thoroughly bad, although all the defects were not immediately apparent, and many of them could have been remedied in a few hours, or even less, if Nelson were to grant the opportunity and Brueys were to have the wit to do so.

But for Nelson to give his opponent time was quite unlikely. Of his thirteen seventy-fours, two were away to leeward on scouting duty necessitated by his lack of frigates, and Troubridge in *Culloden* was astern hampered by a prize, but the kind of battle Nelson immediately visualized could dispense with their services at the start. The enemy was in sight; he must be given no chance to make special preparations, or to slip away again in the night. A quarter of an hour after the French had been sighted the signal was made to prepare for battle, and the fleet headed steadily towards the French fleet, with a fresh breeze right astern. Next came the signal to be ready to anchor by the stern, and then came the signal to attack the van and centre of the enemy. That was all that was necessary by way of preparation. Nelson was about to plunge into action against a powerful enemy and to wrench a crushing victory out of the most trying navigational difficulties by three signals; the impress of his personality and genius upon the magnificent practical ability of his subordinates ensured such a result.

As the sun was setting the English fleet came gliding into the bay. They had no chart of the locality, but, sounding as they came, they swung out past the dangerous ridge of rocks which runs out from Aboukir Island under the sea, came up again on the enemy's side of it, and fell with crushing violence upon his helpless van. It is hard to decide which to admire the more, the seamanship or the daring of that entry into action in unknown shoals, in growing darkness, with the guns of the enemy loaded and waiting for them. The English line had been formed 'as most convenient'. Foley in the *Goliath* led in the place Troubridge should have filled in the regular order.

Still sounding, he realized as the guns opened that there was room inside the French line; he crossed the bows of the French van ship, raking her, and turned between the French and the shore, anchoring beside the second in the line. The next four ships to the *Goliath* followed her round, blasting the French van with consecutive raking broadsides; in ten minutes the two van ships of the French were beaten into mere wrecks. Nelson, coming next, kept to the outside, added the *Vanguard*'s quota of destruction to the *Guerrier* and *Conquérant* and anchored abreast the third in the line. *Minotaur* and *Defence* followed after. The five ships to the windward end of the French line had been torn by the fire of eight English. Two more English ships, arriving in the smoke and darkness, went too far, came under the fire of the powerful and undamaged French centre, and were roughly handled, but remained able to take their part in the tremendous cannonade which continued for over an hour. Troubridge, coming up in hot haste, with a failing wind and in pitch darkness, ran *Culloden* aground on the reef which the others had contrived to clear, and there he stayed all night mad with rage, but his signals and lights were a valuable aid to *Alexander* and *Swiftsure* coming slowly up from south-westward.

Once the battle had begun the French centre and rear could do little save to wait for the English to move down upon them after destroying the van. With the wind blowing straight down the line, they could not move up to the help of the outnumbered ships, even if they had been instantly ready to move, which they were not. Brueys was dead: he could give no orders even if there had been any to give. Soon after the last two English ships of the line came into action and attacked the French centre, *l'Orient*, the French flagship, caught fire. Her crew still worked madly at her guns for some time, but she blew up with an appalling detonation an hour later, leaving the two ships next ahead of her to the concentrated fire of four ships of the English line and a frigate.

Ship by ship the French fleet had been beaten into helplessness. Some of the others had slipped their cables to avoid the explosion of *l'Orient* and were aground on the shoals, dismasted and helpless; a French frigate which had tried to hinder the *Orion*'s passage inside the French line had already preceded them there, torn open by a broadside. But Nelson had been wounded quite early in the battle, though not before he knew that victory was certain. Hit on the forehead by a small missile, blinded, bleeding profusely and badly shaken, he was taken below, but he could not rest, although he was sure at the moment that his wound was mortal. He sent messages to his wife, to Captain Louis; he began to dictate a despatch to Lord St Vincent; and, when it appeared that his secretary's hand shook too much with excitement in the midst of the inferno round them to write, Nelson, left-handed and dizzy, tried to write with his own hand. He was interrupted by Berry, with the news that *l'Orient* was on fire, and had himself brought on deck again to supervise precautionary measures and attempts to rescue the crew. When at last the wretched ship blew up and all danger was past they persuaded him to go below again.

When dawn came three French ships of the line with two frigates were still afloat and had not surrendered. The rest were either dismasted wrecks in the hands of the English or were aground and helpless, a certain prey. The English crews were worn out by a whole night's fierce fighting; the English ships were badly cut up in their rigging. An attack ought to have been made upon the surviving French ships, possibly before dawn came, but Nelson's disablement had not been conducive to such action. His Captains, resolute and skilful though they were, were unable to extract further efforts from their exhausted crews without the stimulus of Nelson's example and orders; they had their limitations. As it was, the three intact French ships wore round out of their shattered line. The rear ship went aground—a sidelight on French seamanship—and was burned by her captain; the other two got away, the only survivors of a fleet of thirteen. Of the remaining eleven, nine were in the hands of the English.

So complete a victory (a 'conquest' as Nelson describes it) was practically unprecedented in naval history. The Armada lost two-thirds only of its numbers in a campaign which altered the whole balance of naval power, and only a small proportion of the loss was due to gunfire. St Vincent left the beaten side numerically stronger than the victors. A considerable Persian fleet escaped from Salamis; a considerable Turkish one, bearing the captured trophies of a flagship, escaped from Lepanto. The first of June and the battles of the Dutch Wars, the Hogue and even Quiberon, were slight victories compared with the Nile in the matter of immediate destruction. Trafalgar was to come near it, but it still only stands rivalled by Tsu-Shima as an example of the annihilation of one fleet by another of approximately equal material force.

When, after long delay, the news of the battle reached London, there was profound joy. The earlier news of Nelson's fruitless return to Syracuse had caused the utmost dissatisfaction. Even experienced naval officers had suspected Nelson of some serious fault. Had the French fleet (as was quite possible) left the Egyptian coast after landing and escaped back to Toulon, Nelson's recall and ruin would certainly have followed, and he might well have been lost to history. As it was, however, the earlier successful evasion of the French fleet was forgotten in the general joy. It was announced in the House of Commons that he was to be created Baron Nelson of the Nile and to be awarded a pension of

£2000. Contrasted with the Earldom which St Vincent had gained for Jervis the reward appeared meagre, and the discrepancy was sharply commented upon. The defence put forward was that Nelson was not a Commander-in-Chief, and no Admiral not holding that position had ever received more than a barony. It was incidentally remarked that Nelson's reputation did not depend upon the honours bestowed upon him, which was correct, but had no connection with the matter under discussion. From Hood we learn that Pitt was dissuaded from rewarding Nelson with a Viscountcy, but by whom and with what motive Hood's letter tantalizingly refuses to disclose. The Admiralty's letter to Nelson seems to accuse itself while excusing itself, pointing out apologetically that the addition of the words 'of the Nile' to his title was an unprecedented distinction. Nelson, who had confidently expected an Earldom, replied with a moderation most surprising; his wording of the letter leads one to suspect him of dissimulation and sarcasm quite foreign to his style.

CHAPTER X

NAPLES

THE immediate fruit of victory was the unchallenged supremacy of the British fleet in the Eastern Mediterranean; and the arrival, at last, of the frigates which had been pursuing him as long as he had been pursuing the French enabled Nelson to make that supremacy felt. A blockade of the Egyptian coast promptly raised unending difficulties for the French army and reduced Alexandria (until then dependent on sea-borne supplies) to a condition of semi-starvation. The French in Egypt lost all hope of reinforcement or succour. Whatever schemes Bonaparte may have meditated upon Constantinople were now restricted to attacks by land over the difficult desert route with his flank ever exposed to counter-attack by sea. A warning sent to the Governor of Bombay by Nelson overland from Alexandretta ensured that precautions would be taken in Indian waters to prevent any reinforcement of Tippoo Sahib by the French via the Red Sea.

In the midst of making these arrangements the equally urgent one of refitting the fleet and prizes had to be carried on. Nelson was very ill and shaken by his wound—a letter of his to St Vincent says that on the day the despatches about the Nile were sent off he was attacked by a fever and his life despaired of for eighteen hours. It was probably his old enemy malaria appearing again (it must have gained a firm grip of his system at San Juan and Bastia), but the blow on his forehead had also much to do with it, and most likely the relief from the extreme nervous tension of the past eight weeks left him weak and unstrung. He was vomiting continually—a bad symptom after a head wound—and he attributes the speed with which the fleet was refitted on a hostile coast with no base at hand solely to the exertions of Troubridge, Ball, Hood and Hallowell. Yet despite the illness of which he complains he got through an enormous amount of work, writing a great bulk of private and official letters during this period, many of them of the kind one expects of Nelson—anxious letters to make sure that Troubridge should receive reward for the Nile along with the other captains despite *Culloden*'s running on the reef, letters to make sure that the fleet will receive the prize money for the prizes he had had to burn because of the difficulty of refitting them, letters to his agent arranging for his relations to share in his Nile pension. He did so much, indeed, that we are led to suspect that the illness of which he writes was not as serious as he describes it—or else that his energy of mind was so great as to make negligible weakness of his body. All the same, there begin to creep into his correspondence hints which later are to become a recurrent and pronounced *motif* in his letters. The first is to be found soon after the battle— 'I feel I must soon leave my situation up the Mediterranean'.

Some of the prizes were burnt; some patched up and sent back to Gibraltar or England. Captain Hood, in the *Zealous*, was left in command of two ships of the line and three frigates to maintain the blockade of the Egyptian and Syrian coasts, and he himself with the three worst damaged ships of the line set off down the Mediterranean. 'I detest this voyage', he wrote. 'Nothing but absolute necessity could force

me to the measure.' And the port whither he was bound for
was Naples!

Here he arrived on September 22nd, announcing that he
was only going to stay a few days to patch up the battered
Vanguard, and certain, at the moment, that the best base for
his future operations would be Syracuse. A week later he was
still of the same mind, looking forward to getting to sea,
sending to St Vincent his historic denunciation of Naples as
a country of 'fiddlers and poets, whores and scoundrels'.

But the victory of the Nile had been a potent factor in the
moulding of international opinion. The new Coalition which
England was so patiently building up had taken form. Austria
was inclined to reopen the struggle. The weak-minded Czar
was sending Suvarof and an army to take part in the war in
northern Italy. The Kingdom of Naples, trembling before the
steady advance of French military and political influence in
the peninsula, was inclined now to oppose it by force. The
news of the battle which had freed the country from the fear
of a naval descent was received with the utmost joy; honours
and rewards, including the Dukedom of Bronté in Sicily,
were heaped upon Nelson, and his birthday, the week after
his arrival, was the occasion of magnificent fêtes and illuminations in all the beautiful bay. The tottering Bourbon
monarchy lived in renewed hope of rolling back the republican tide.

The person in Naples who was most overjoyed, however,
was no Italian, but an Englishwoman born and bred. She was
a very tall and massive woman, who with the slow advance of
the years had put on flesh (not, however, to an alarming
extent at present), so that she quite dwarfed the lean little
Nelson when she stood beside him. Her past was not of a
type to bear much inspection. A Cheshire girl of poor
parents, she had passed through various men's hands, bear-

ing an illegitimate child, but had received the protection of Charles Greville, the pattern of the perfect prig, while still quite young. He set himself to educate her, and he undoubtedly did much to improve her knowledge of society and its conventions, while her natural good taste found more outlet for its expression. The educational process lasted long after Greville had passed out of her life, for we can note in her letters a steady improvement in her spelling and her grammar. She was certainly both quick and willing to learn, especially under the stimulus of the passion which Greville inspired, for during the four years of Greville's tuition, she learnt to love him very dearly. But Greville had an uncle, Sir William Hamilton, a polished diplomat of the old school, with a nice taste in antiques, whose purchase of the Portland Vase (with an eye, it is true, to subsequent profit) would have given him a pleasant though not conspicuous place in history had not his subsequent marriage condemned him to another, comparable with that held by Mr Beeton and other husbands. Sir William's wife had died during the period of Emma's tuition, making it exceeding likely that Sir William's nephew, Greville, would be his heir, and Sir William owned a nice piece of property round about Pembroke which only needed attention and the expenditure of a little capital to become very valuable. It was to Greville's interest that Sir William should not remarry, and it happened that after Hamilton had returned to Naples after a brief leave in England Emma was sent out to him, while the Pembroke property passed into Greville's care. It may sound incredible (although it is not the least incredible part of Emma's story), but at Naples for some time Hamilton's interest in her was purely avuncular; he saw to her instruction in music (her ear was never quite true) and Italian, and in courtly behaviour, until at last Greville's written commands to her were obeyed and she

yielded to Sir William's solicitations—in payment, seemingly, for Sir William's making a will in Greville's favour.

It seems as if Emma never truly loved Sir William, but she
was a talented woman and made him happy. She had blossomed out in security, she was very beautiful and her artistic
taste was well trained by Sir William. The best Neapolitan
society acknowledged her existence, and Emma managed
things so well that on Sir William's next leave in England the
pair were married, although he received a sharp rebuff on
attempting to introduce her into English Court circles. Back
at Naples again, however, there was no similar difficulty. Sir
William and Lady Hamilton were received everywhere; even
English noblewomen called on her; soon she was well in the
good graces of that masterful woman, Maria Carolina, Queen
of Naples. Seeing that the King was much more interested
in the wholesale slaughter of game than in the government
of his country, which Acton and the Queen shared in an
undetermined fashion, this meant that Emma had a good
deal of influence in the formation of what, for lack of a better term, must be called the Neapolitan policy. To Emma,
Naples meant much. It offered her a social position denied
her at home, and of an eminence far superior to anything she
could hope to attain at home. Sincerely fond of the Queen,
her views naturally resembled those of that lady, to whom,
naturally, a republican was utterly abhorrent. The subjection
of Naples by the French would be to Emma a crushing disaster, just as the defeat of France by Europe would be a reason
for rejoicing. Emma's political opinions, however, were on a
narrow scale; British successes were a cause of joy, but not
more than that. Naples was her main concern. And one other
side of her character it is well to notice: she had a thirst for
glory and celebrity. She had little taste for power—she
wielded ample power in Naples—and little for wealth.

Glory—even reflected glory—was what she wanted. Celebrity—or notoriety as a substitute—came a good second, with other passions far behind.

Naples had been in a state of frightful anxiety after Nelson's second departure from Sicily. She was exposed and friendless, and her considerate treatment of Nelson's fleet might bring upon her terrible maltreatment by the French. The French representative ('the regicide minister', as Emma called him) had been profuse in threats and protests, borne up by the knowledge that Bonaparte was loose on the seas with a fleet and an army. The arrival of the *Mutine* with the news of the Nile altered all this. Citizen Garrat changed his tone. The Queen fell into hysterical delight; Emma went one better and fell down in a faint, bruising herself. Nelson's arrival took place when the enthusiasm had reached its full height. Lady Hamilton wore blue shawls dotted with anchors; 'sonets on sonets' (as she spelled it) were written in Nelson's praise; it was clear that Nelson was the greatest hero she had ever met, and the closer she was to him the larger would be her share of the limelight. She fainted again with joy when she went on board the *Vanguard*, and Nelson caught her falling bulk with his one arm—a faint as genuine as her enthusiasm; her desire for the limelight was a quite unconscious passion.

Some time before she had written, 'We are preparing your apartment against you come,' and it was with the Hamiltons that Nelson took up his residence while he plunged abruptly into Neapolitan politics. He found that Sir William was ageing fast, and was not the man he had been at the time of their first meeting in 1793. His wife attended to much of his business—her close connection with the Queen made it certain that she would—and it was to her that Nelson turned when he wanted things done. We find him writing to her, formally but indignantly, about Neapolitan apathy. He was a sick, wounded man, something of a *malade imaginaire*, too, just come through a period of intense anxiety—exactly as Emma had. She could pay him that womanly attention for which even Ball's devotion and even Troubridge's affection were poor substitutes. She could heap flattery upon him, which was none the less fulsome because it was sincere, and by a trick of his mental make-up he very much liked fulsome flattery. His wife had given him just praise and no more. She had been attentive to him—but the years he had spent with her had been the bitter ones of retirement and neglect, plus the few anguished months of recovery from his wound. Emma's ample beauty and her superb carriage and her position as disperser of the Royal largesse had won her immediate popularity in the service and the title of 'Patroness of the Navy'. With so many tastes in common, with so much on each side desired and to be given, it is hardly to be wondered at that they were soon in each other's arms. He had no eye for her faults; his life had been passed on the sea or with his wife; his knowledge of women was limited to his knowledge of Lady Nelson and of his idealised mental pictures of Lady Parker, Mrs Moutray and their successors. He could form no idea of the narrowness of her mental outlook or the exiguousness of her talents. In three weeks at Naples a genuine affection had blossomed between them.

For a time they were parted. Nelson sailed with the *Vanguard* and other ships to form the blockade of Malta. Gozo fell to the English, and Captain Ball was left to raise revolt among the Maltese, encouraged by lavish promises of Neapolitan assistance. The newly-arrived Portuguese squadron had to have its duties in the blockade allotted to it, and its officers reconciled to an English command. Arrangements had to be made to make the most use of

Turkey's tardy entry into the war with France. The revict-ualling and refitting of the rest of the squadron needed attention, and a sharp eye kept on the French arrangements at Toulon for the relief of Malta. But it was all done in a week, and Nelson was back again at Naples; forgotten, apparently, was his recent vow to make Syracuse his base of operations.

The reason was soon apparent, if not the cause. Nelson had promised the Royal family never to leave Naples without the support of the English fleet—one ship of the line of it, at least—whose guns could be relied upon to put down rebellion or drive off French raiders, whose presence was a valuable outward demonstration to the discontented of England's support, and upon whose decks, at least, the King and Queen and the Royal treasure could be certain of sanc-tuary. Moreover, as it grew obvious that soon Austria would be at war again with France, Nelson felt a vast yearning to strike the first blow. There were sixty thousand Neapolitan troops at hand, under a general of repute; Nelson, although he could see (and bitterly complain about) the corruption of the Government, did not appreciate the facts that two-thirds of the men in the ranks were raw recruits and that Mack was a spiritless nincompoop. Fifteen thousand French were in occupation of Rome, and to Nelson's respect for long-established authority this was a continual affront. Fifty thousand Neapolitans, aided by the diversions the English fleet would make in the French rear, should drive the French from Rome and penetrate into northern Italy and drag Austria into hostilities at once. He was now, formally, one of the King's advisers, and in Council he pressed hotly for immediate war. The presence of an officer of a belligerent state on the council of a neutral one was a little odd, but Nelson never seemed to appreciate the oddness—English

Admirals in those days of poor communications had some strange responsibilities thrust upon them occasionally. Warning came of Austria's unreadiness, but that was disregarded. Nelson's advice carried the day, and the army was despatched northwards to destroy the hated French, to bring down in ruins the abominally-named Roman Republic, to root out the Trees of Liberty and similar symbols of perversion—and, incidentally, to see if a few unconsidered trifles of territory might not come the way of the Bourbon monarchy. It proved to be as ill-considered a movement as the Roumanian declaration of war in 1916.

Nelson took five thousand men on board, and landed them at Leghorn, which surrendered at once. Troubridge was left to re-establish the old Riviera blockade, and to attack the coastal shipping. Nelson came back to Naples, to receive the welcome news that Rome (save for St Angelo) was in the hands of the Neapolitans, and that Mack was leading twenty thousand men (gross mismanagement, starvation, dysentery and desertion had already thinned the ranks appallingly) to attack the French in their prepared position at Civita Castellana. Four days later came new tidings. Mack had divided his forces, and bad staff work had ruined his attack. The Neapolitans had broken and fled except when they had gone bodily over to the French. Mack and a tiny relic of the army was in retreat on Naples, with the French treading on their heels.

The consternation was terrible. The Royal family was distracted with apprehension. Everywhere in the kingdom the revolutionary movement raised its head. Naples itself was torn between demonstrations of loyalty and desperate plottings of the republicans. Working hand in hand, Nelson and Lady Hamilton sought to save something from the inevitable wreck. The Royal treasures were sent on board labelled as

'naval stores'. For twelve days the Royal family had repeatedly to appear on the palace balcony, and, bowing and smil-
ing, to assure the suspicious *lazzaroni* of their continued
presence. Then a magnificent reception was held to cele-
brate the investiture by the Turkish Minister of Nelson with
the Plume of Honour decreed him by the Sultan. After the
reception the King and Queen and their children, their
attendants, the English Minister and his wife and various
other diplomats, crept out of the palace, armed to the teeth
and carrying dark lanterns, down to the quay by the arsenal
and to the safety of the *Vanguard*'s protection. She sailed for
Palermo on the 23rd December, 1799; on the 23rd January,
1800, the French entered Naples.

On his own authority Nelson had inveigled a neutral
power into a war which had promptly brought down upon it
a crushing disaster. It was a bad mistake. Actually, he had
much to excuse him. He could plead that Mack's fifty thousand men should have swept the meagre French forces
before them. He had at least gained an ally for England. But
before he assumed the responsibility of sending Mack into
action he should have ascertained whether Mack and his
men were fit for their task; he believed, after inspection,
that they were, but no naval officer is able to form a reliable
opinion about the merits of a national army. He had gained
the active alliance of the Sicilian part of the kingdom, but at
the cost of the loss of the benevolent neutrality of the
Neapolitan part, which was of extreme value. Worst of all, he
had demonstrated that England could not protect any
European country whither French troops could march.

Briefly, Nelson had been guilty of an error of judgment in
failing to appreciate the possibilities of the Roman campaign, and that error can be ascribed primarily to his rashness
in involving himself in military affairs, and secondarily

(perhaps, but very likely) to the bias Lady Hamilton's views had given to his opinions. That his later opinions were biased in that manner cannot be doubted. The same seems to hold good in this case. He had been influenced by the Neapolitan hatred of the French revolutionary ideas, and equally so by Neapolitan optimism—both as represented to him by Lady Hamilton.

A little delay, as events were to prove, would have seen the entry of Austrian and Russian troops into northern Italy and the evacuation of the southern end of the Peninsula by the French. The Neapolitans would then have had the same glory of the occupation of Rome and Leghorn without any of the subsequent disasters and massacres and loss of British prestige.

CHAPTER XI

PALERMO

THE voyage was prolonged by a terrible and sudden storm. It took over three days of severe hardship to reach Palermo, during which the wretched Italians gave themselves up for lost. On Christmas Day the youngest prince, Albert, died in Lady Hamilton's arms. Sir William spent his time sitting with a loaded pistol ready to save himself from the pains of drowning, not even reconciled by the thought that he had saved his precious vases from the contamination of a French touch. Of all the hapless civilians Lady Hamilton was the only one to display nerve and spirit, nursing the whole Royal family single-handed. Small wonder that on their eventual arrival at Palermo the Bourbons clung more desperately to her than ever. They needed help in this business of settling down in their island possessions and of trying to arrange for a counter-offensive against the French, who, welcomed by the aristocratic class of republicans, had set up a Parthenopeian Republic in Naples with all the trappings of tricolour flags and trees of liberty which irritated Nelson so profoundly.

He had, indeed, much to vex him. Ball in Malta had performed wonders. With only a small landing force he had roused the islanders, armed and equipped them as well as he could, and had penned the French garrison into Valetta. But his numbers were barely large enough, and the men he had were shoeless and starving as a result of the failure of the Sicilian Government to keep their promises. Nelson wrote letter after letter, and had interview after interview with Acton, trying to extract from him something more substantial than promises. He obtained a few hundred troops—and, seeing how scarce soldiers were after the disasters of the autumn, that was an achievement—but the civil service was in such a muddled condition that although supplies were to be had, and shipping was available to carry them, and British gold to pay for them, they could not be moved in time— Troubridge, when in command of the blockading squadron, actually had later to send into Girgenti and requisition corn by main force.

During this interval of stress arrived the news that the Government in London had made one of the clumsiest and most tactless moves that ever a civilian government in charge of a war had succeeded in devising. They sent a junior naval captain and his brother as joint ambassadors to Turkey, and at the same time gave the former orders to act against the French in Syria and Egypt, all this without informing Nelson, who was actually engaged upon, and responsible for, operations in this quarter, as well as in constant correspondence with the Turks and the Russians, who were naturally deeply interested in the proceedings. Worst of all, this Ambassador-Captain was Sir Sydney Smith, who was responsible for the failure (which he had contrived to gloss over at home) to destroy the French naval material at Toulon in 1793. Nelson had no great opinion of his talents, and none of his trustworthiness, and he was exasperated beyond all measure by Smith's cool assumption that Hood's squadron acting off Alexandria should come under his orders. Troubridge, senior to Smith, was sent off in haste to take command there and bring the ships off, leaving the blockade to Smith's squadron. St Vincent backed Nelson up, but the feeling of soreness remained—it was expressed in a hope that he might retire, and be conveyed in the *Vanguard* to England with his friends, Sir William and Lady Hamilton, and the matter recurs again and again in letters, where Nelson vainly endeavours to discover whether it is the Ambassador or the Captain who is addressing him, and asks Smith only to communicate ministerial affairs 'jointly with your respectable brother', because an Ambassador can give such directions, and in such a form to an Admiral as would be highly improper for a Captain to employ. Smith's services, at Acre and elsewhere, were, as it turned out, far more successful than Nelson had ever thought they would be, but there was a continual clash between the two in consequence of Smith's desire (a result of his diplomatic position) to re-establish Turkish rule in Egypt at any cost, even that of giving the French free passage to France, while Nelson was most anxious to keep them there until sickness and casualties forced an unconditional surrender.

While all this was going on Nelson was living in the Hamilton's house at Palermo. It must be remembered that it was highly inconvenient to a one-armed man to live on board ship when he was likely to be constantly required to interview important officials on land, but it was an inadequate excuse; equally inadequate was the excuse that he must be in constant touch with the representative of the British Government. He had grown desperately fond of the Hamiltons—both of them—and they were fond of him. His system had grown accustomed to, and now stood in constant need of, the dangerous drug of fulsome flattery which Lady Hamilton dispensed to him in such quantity. He was good-natured, altruistic, an idealist; we find him, who had so long been accustomed to going to bed at ten and rising at five, sitting up at card parties until morning, losing his money without much interest (he had kept away from gambling since his youth), backing Lady Hamilton's play, or allowing her a free hand to play with his money. About them were gathered all the shady characters the Sicilian Court could show—and they were many—and the loose living and the heavy drinking of the Hamiltons' friends soon became notorious, and Nelson's reputation was fast becoming tainted by the wild gossip which was spread by the English visitors to Palermo. Troubridge had the courage to write to Nelson telling him of what was being said, and begging him to get away to sea, but Nelson was convinced by now that his most important duty was the supervision of affairs in the Two Sicilies, which he could only attend to in person. So he stayed on at Palermo, at the Hamiltons' house, drawn closer and closer to both of them, but more—much more—to Emma, whose husband, appointed to Naples in the dear pre-Revolutionary days when the post was more decorative than active, was finding all this stress of war and revolution too severe for him in his old age.

Nelson flung himself energetically into the business of the reconquest of Naples. In March Troubridge returned from Alexandria, and was promptly sent off to the Bay of Naples to blockade the place and reduce the islands in the bay. That remarkable man, Ruffo, who was a Cardinal without being a priest, had landed in Calabria with a Christian army (so it was entitled) made up of galley slaves and the sweepings of the Sicilian gaols, and was encouraging the insurrection of Calabria, which had already displayed itself in the murder of Republic officials and the ambushing of French detachments. The French army was far too weak to hold down the Neapolitan dominions—the French advance to

Naples had been a serious mistake, in fact—and all they could do was to garrison the important fortresses, hold the town of Naples quiet, and await either reinforcements from France or the attack of any force Sicily could raise and the sea power of Britain convey. The peasantry rapidly rose for their King—which seems to indicate, unless the pinch of blockade had already influenced them, that the precipitate flight to Palermo was a mistake—and soon the French were all hemmed in behind walls, such of them as had not been hurriedly summoned north to repair the disasters there brought about by the victories of Suvaroff. Troubridge was soon in possession, not only of the islands in the bay, but also of various places on the mainland. Yet at this very moment, when King Ferdinand was only waiting cannily for the complete reconquest of his dominions to make a solemn re-entry into Naples, arrived fresh news of the utmost moment.

Twenty-five ships of the line had escaped from Brest, and had reached the Mediterranean. French anxiety about the force in Egypt, and English naval pressure on the French and Italian coasts, had been too intense for the Paris Government to bear, and this fleet had been sent round in an attempt to relieve the tension. Nelson instantly sent out orders to his ships to concentrate. Troubridge came down from Naples, the Portuguese came up from Malta. Nelson was greatly worried about leaving no English ship at the disposition of the Neapolitan Court, but he nerved himself to break his promise to the Queen. With his ships concentrated off Maritimo (an island west of the western extremity of Sicily), he awaited further news, prepared, if Duckworth from Minorca joined him, to oppose the nineteen French (that was the estimate he had received) with fourteen English and Portuguese. Nelson's position here covered Sicily as well as the blockade of Alexandria; his main concern was lest a French force should land in Sicily, which in that case might have been lost to the cause as promptly as Naples was. The news came that the French had reached Toulon, with St Vincent after them with sixteen of the line, and Nelson promptly re-established the blockade of Malta. Duckworth came next, with four ships, and among them was the *Foudroyant*, 80, which had long ago been designed for Nelson's flagship and to which he now transferred his flag. Berry, who had been captured in the *Leander* on the way home with the Nile despatches and since exchanged, was his flag-captain.

St Vincent at Port Mahon now directed, for the short time remaining before his going home on sick leave, the operations of two fleets—Keith's with twenty ships of the line off Toulon, and Nelson's sixteen off Sicily, which Nelson now brought back to Palermo. Keith found the French fleet, lost it again, and sent two ships to reinforce Nelson, as both he and Nelson were firmly convinced that the French were determined on the relief of Naples. Nelson, who was just preparing to convey two thousand Sicilians and the Crown Prince to that town, was furious at the paucity of the reinforcement. With eighteen sail of the line, all two deckers, all of them short of men, three of them Portuguese, and one only a sixty-four, he was expected to fight Bruix with twenty-two, four of them three-deckers. He refused to sail in search of the French. He declared that if the fleets were to meet, the French would be too badly cut up in the battle to do any further harm, while the English might not lose a ship, but the odds were too great to seek a battle, although he pointed out that in England people would only hear that he had refused a battle of eighteen against twenty-two. However, the situation cleared up. The French stayed on the Riviera coast, and twelve more ships arrived from England at

Minorca. The despatch with this news also informed Nelson that St Vincent was going home, leaving Keith, the senior officer, in command in the Mediterranean. Nelson, relieved of anxiety, promptly hurried to Naples.

There was, in Nelson's opinion, need to haste. Rumours had reached him that the French and rebel troops in the fortresses of the town had entered into negotiations with Ruffo, and were offering to surrender the places on condition of being sent to France. Such capitulation was, to Nelson's mind, monstrous. The rebels against whom he cherished such a bitter animosity should be put on trial, and should not have a chance given them of aiding the French further. The French should become prisoners of war. He dashed to Naples from Palermo; he had with him Sir William and Lady Hamilton, but he had not waited either for the Crown Prince or the troops; it would have been better for his reputation, perhaps, if he had.

He found rumour correct on his arrival. Ruffo had made terms with the rebels, and Captain Foote, the senior English naval officer present, had signed with him. Ruffo had been expressly forbidden to make such terms, and Foote had no authority to do so. Nelson, using the authority delegated him by the King, promptly annulled the capitulation, despite Ruffo's and Foote's protests, and demanded unconditional surrender, backing the demand with the display of his eighteen ships of the line ready for action. It was enough. The rebels in Uovo and Nuovo surrendered unconditionally.

If all this is correct there was nothing dishonourable about Nelson's actions. They were a little odd at first glance, because he acted throughout as an English naval officer, and made no mention of the powers he held from the King of Naples, so that it might be thought he was high-handedly interfering in Neapolitan business, but actually he was

directing it, along the lines authorized by the highest
Neapolitan authority. But it is generally assumed that at the
time of his arrival the armistice had begun to take effect, so
that the rebels were out of their strong places, and helpless,
in which case the most Nelson could do would be to put
them back again and start new negotiations. There is direct
authority for the belief that affairs were in this state;
Hamilton's Foreign Office despatch says so. But Hamilton
was old, his knowledge of military affairs was scanty, and his
report is directly contradicted in this and other matters of
fact by the logs of the *Foudroyant* and the *Seahorse* and by
other good evidence. Hamilton's report, written over a fortnight after the event, can therefore be set aside in favour of
the other evidence. Nelson was quite within his rights in
annulling the capitulation, and he gained no unfair advantage by so doing, and not one of his decisions savoured of
sharp practice.

The mistake he made, of course, was in being mixed up in
the business at all. The fine distinction between a British
Admiral holding incidental authority from the King of
Naples, and an agent of the King holding incidental rank in
the British Navy, was lost on the general public. All the public saw was a British officer seizing Neapolitan rebels and
delivering them up to the horrible ferocity of the Bourbons.
Bourbon hangmen and Bourbon gaols between them made
short work of the wretched rebels; the monarchy had had a
nasty fright, and took its revenge with all the blind venom of
conscious weakness and all the cruelty of a degenerate
government. Ruffo's main motive, indeed, in making the
terms he had offered, was to get the unfortunates out of the
reach of the Bourbons. Nelson's main motive was to see that
they did not escape. Such was his hatred of the republicans
that he did not think the dreadful treatment meted out by

Ferdinand's henchmen a whit too bad for them. It seems
nowadays very bad taste, if nothing worse. But Lady
Hamilton agreed with him.

Among those executed was Francesco Caracciolo, a man of
forty-seven, who, after distinguished service with the
Bourbons, had joined the republicans, had acted as their
minister of marine, had commanded vessels in action against
the loyal fleet, had assisted in the defence of the forts, and
had finally been taken prisoner when in hiding in the country. He was tried, at Nelson's order, by a court-martial of
Neapolitan officers, found guilty and hanged, all on the same
day as he was brought on board the *Foudroyant*. At the time
of the execution Nelson was at dinner with the Hamiltons
and Lord Northwich. Those are the bare facts of the case,
and Southey's and the other condemnations of the execution
as a judicial murder seem to be at fault. Caracciolo was
undoubtedly guilty—we have Troubridge's and Foote's
letters of May, 1799, when he was in action against them, to
prove it—and whether he was tried by personal enemies or
not—which remains doubtful—he suffered in the end only
the penalty he knowingly incurred. The other horrible lies in
circulation about Lady Hamilton having, in company with
Nelson, gloated over the hanging are disproved by Lord
Northwich's and others' evidence—Brenton, for instance,
represents her as addressing Nelson by a title not given him
till some time later. Yet once again the spectacle of an
English officer concerning himself with the judicial executions of the Neapolitan Government is unpleasing, and the
haste with which Caracciolo was disposed of—unnecessary,
now that the rebellion was ended—was positively indecent.

Next day the King arrived in the bay—all personal danger
being now at an end—and the *Foudroyant* displayed the
strange spectacle of being at once the flagship of an English

Admiral, the palace of a King, and the official residence of an English Minister and his wife. From the *Foudroyant* were issued the Royal decrees which arranged for the slaughter of the rebels. The French garrison in St Elmo, hard pressed, surrendered on terms. Only Capua and Gaeta (the latter one of the strongest fortresses in Europe) remained in French hands, and the Sicilian troops moved against them. But after recent events it would be a rash man who would trust Sicilian levies against disciplined forces and powerful fortifications. Something must be done to stiffen them. Nelson landed a thousand seamen under Troubridge for the purpose, and the siege of Capua, twenty miles inland, was begun.

Already Nelson had had warning from Keith that should the French break out from Toulon he would be required to reinforce Keith off Minorca, and already he had decided on his course of action. Immediately after came the news that the French had come out, and with the news came positive orders to send ships. Nelson did not do so. Orders more explicit followed, requiring all, or at least the greater part, of Nelson's squadron, to sail for Minorca. Nelson refused flatly. In his opinion it was better to stay by Naples than to join Keith, although he knew that the French had joined the Spaniards at Cartagena and had now forty ships against Keith's thirty-one. It was largely Keith's fault that the enemy had been able to unite without a battle; but that nominally did not affect the matter. Nelson had no knowledge which Keith lacked; all that he was doing was asserting his own opinion against that of his superior officer, which is an exceedingly dangerous thing to do and needs much justification. Keith would have been within his rights if he had sent Nelson home.

As events turned out, the allied fleets neither sought battle nor came to Naples, but dashed out of the Mediterranean with Keith behind them and eventually took refuge in Brest, where they were once more blockaded. Perhaps if Nelson had been with Keith they might have been caught, and certainly Nelson's eighteen ships of the line were of small use where they were—except that they were providing the men whose employment at Capua was most effective.

That was the cause of the trouble. Nelson was unable to give Keith effective help even if he wanted to, with so many men inland beyond immediate recall. Expecting, as he did, orders to sail at any moment, he had no business in sending so many men away, although he pleaded their absence as an excuse for staying. The Admiralty rapped him sharply over the knuckles for his actions, laying down certain excellent rules regarding the employment of a naval landing force. Trained sailors are as good, perhaps, as soldiers on land, but they are very hard to replace, and their loss should only be risked for an adequate naval object. If a disaster in the field had cut off the landing force it would have been as great a blow as the loss of a naval action—and Capua could not be considered worth that price. Nelson had thought so; but he had lived with the Hamiltons for some months now, and his valuation of Naples was inflated far beyond exactness. The severity of the Admiralty letters caused Nelson deep sorrow—he was as sensitive to reproof as he was to flattery—but no official action was taken beyond that. Even in those days it was possible for an officer to have more prestige than a government, and it seems doubtful if any ministry could have stood the strain of sending the victor of the Nile before a court-martial. A later government was to flinch at recalling Sir Douglas Haig after Paschendaele.

For six months now there was no great naval event in the Mediterranean. Nelson was left in command there by the Admiralty in Keith's absence, and he could busy himself with controlling at a distance all the multifarious operations in that sea: the blockades of Syria, Alexandria and Malta; the pacification of Southern Italy; convoys; the finding of troops to attack La Valetta; the disposal of his small force so as to make most economical use of it; the inducing of the Portuguese squadron to remain, contrary to orders, on their station. Capua and Gaeta fell speedily, thanks to the energy of Troubridge, who established his batteries close to the walls and took full advantage of the drooping spirits of the French garrisons, cut off from all hope of succour. In the north the wild energy of Suvaroff was conquering all Lombardy and Piedmont. Disaster followed disaster for the French arms. Rome, evacuated by the French troops on their way to their defeat at the Trebbia, fell to the boats of Captain Louis's squadron, which rowed up the Tiber, fulfilling a quaint prophecy that Nelson's ships should take Rome.

News of triumphs were arriving daily at Palermo, where still the *Foudroyant* swung idly at anchor, having returned from Naples. On her deck the lovely Lady Hamilton played her harp and captured the admiration of susceptible midshipmen—she was sure of Nelson's by now. Court circles, intoxicated with victory, lived more lavishly than ever. In August, with vast pomp, amid circumstances as impressive as possible, the King bestowed upon Nelson the title of Duke of Bronté, and with it an estate which was declared to be worth £3000 a year. That was what the Neapolitans said, actually it was a piece of church property sequestered by the Crown a century before, and left to go to ruin since that time. The nearest road passed it by at a distance of forty miles, so that its products reached the market with difficulty, and the tenants had lost the habit of paying rent. To his dying hour Nelson was always a little doubtful as to what income the place could bring him in, and he seems never to have received very much from it, although when he heard of its value from the Neapolitans he promptly settled £500 a year as a first charge upon its income for his father. The gambling and the excitement of social life in Palermo continued as madly as ever. Poor old Sir William found that his wife was losing much money at the green cloth, while he heard from England that Greville's Pembroke schemes had not yet come to fruition and demanded the prompt outlay of further large sums if the whole business were not to end in loss. What with the cost of Greville's development schemes, Lady Hamilton's gambling losses, and the inordinate expense of his household, poor Sir William began to find himself hard pressed for money; it was not long, indeed, before he was actually in Nelson's debt for a considerable sum, which increased to £2000 before their return to England. But no one seemed to care at present. Life was a feverish dream.

Nelson was not even roused from the dream by the action of the Admiralty in sending Keith back to the Mediterranean as Commander-in-Chief. He had hoped for the appointment himself, although still only a Rear-Admiral, and had, indeed, for some time been carrying out its duties without either the staff or the emoluments attached to the post. He was embittered by the news, especially now that further information had shown that Keith had missed a splendid chance of catching Bruix the year before. There would have been a serious quarrel between the two had Keith chosen to indulge in one. But he made good-humoured allowance for the cantankerousness of his junior, as far as his solid ideas of discipline allowed, although he was seriously annoyed at the length of Nelson's stay in Palermo. On more than one occasion—crowning shame—Nelson had shifted his flag to a transport or storeship in the harbour; there had been active employment for every ship of the line under Nelson's command, but

Nelson had found none for himself. It does not sound at all
like Nelson, but it was true. He was very much beglamoured
by his new friends.

Keith broke into the distorted muddle at last. He
summoned Nelson to join him at Leghorn, and then accompanied him in the *Queen Charlotte* from Leghorn, first back to
Palermo, where he endured eight days of 'fulsome vanity and
absurdity' before he haled his fretful subordinate off to the
blockade of Malta. The blockade had endured sixteen
months; for four Nelson had not been near the island. Yet on
the instant of his arrival a relieving force from Toulon made
its appearance. The *Foudroyant*, hard driven, caught a ship of
the line, after a frigate had cut up her rigging, and captured
her in a fierce duel, the French Rear-Admiral on board dying
of his wounds, while the other vessels of the squadron failed
in their attempt to gain Valetta. Nelson plumed himself on
having effected this capture after disobeying Keith's orders,
but it seems likely, in view of Keith's report, that a signal was
misread and that actually Nelson was fulfilling his wishes.
The ship taken was the *Généreux*, one of the two which had
escaped from the Nile; the other was in Valetta, threatened
by the siege of the town and blockaded by the squadron. To
crown his great achievement of the Nile the capture of this
last ship, the *Guillaume Tell*, alone remained, and Keith left
Nelson with the earnest request that he should remain and
see the matter through. He himself was summoned north, to
co-operate once more with the Austrians on the Riviera coast,
where Massena's defence of Genoa was about to begin.

Keith sailed north on the 24th February, 1800; the very
next day Nelson was writing to Hamilton that he found difficulty in getting out of the situation in which he found himself, but, by implication, he wanted to do so. On March 8th
he was writing to Keith to say that his health was so indif-

ferent that he was obliged to retire to Palermo for a few weeks—Keith's orders had expressly laid down Syracuse as the rendezvous for the blockading squadron—and on the 10th he sailed. Fortunately he sent back the *Foudroyant* on his arrival, hoisting his flag once more on a transport. The *Foudroyant* returned just in time to catch the *Guillaume Tell*, which came out in a desperate attempt to reach France, and, well handled and fought with fierce courage, actually shook off some of her pursuers before the *Foudroyant* came in range. Had the *Guillaume Tell* made her attempt a few days earlier and succeeded in consequence of the *Foudroyant's* absence the result to Nelson could not have failed to be serious. His good luck still held, even though it was beginning to be undeserved.

Keith had already written guardedly to Nelson expressing regret at Nelson's return to Palermo, but the Admiralty, Lord Spencer in particular in a private letter, were more outspoken, asking why he did not come home if he was unfit to cruise off Malta. But the letter crossed one from Nelson which asked for recall on the grounds of ill-health.

Some time before, Lord Elgin had stayed a week at Palermo on his way to Constantinople to take up the Ambassadorship to the Porte, which was to result in the despatch to London of the frieze of the Parthenon. Seemingly he had reported home on Sir William's condition; he may have pointed out that the affairs of England in Naples were being left in the hands of Lady Hamilton. In April, 1800, arrived the order for Hamilton's recall and at the same time arrived Sir A Paget to take up Hamilton's duties. In April, 1800, Nelson became as anxious to leave Palermo as previously he had been to go there. He did not even wish to stay to receive the capitulation of Malta, for whose blockade he had been responsible for a year and a half.

Two days after Hamilton had presented his letters of
recall, he, his wife and Nelson went off for a five weeks'
cruise in the *Foudroyant*—a pleasure cruise largely, although
off Malta they came under the distant fire of the long-range
guns mounted in Valetta. And during this cruise something
else happened. Obscure references creep into Nelson's
jocose private letters to Emma after this date. There can be
no doubting that from this time onward Nelson was unfaith-
ful to his wife and Emma to her husband.

Until fairly recently there was room for doubt. The purity
of the relations between the queer pair was hotly maintained
by champion after champion. By some it was even covertly
suggested that their relations were pure of necessity, and
that Nelson's request for a knighthood instead of a baronetcy
after St Vincent was due to his inability to have children to
inherit the latter honour. But now that Nelson's letters to
Emma are available, and can be read by those who take the
trouble, it cannot be doubted that both the one theory and
the other are faulty, and that Nelson was guilty of an offence
against Sir William's hospitality. After all, Emma and Nelson
had been living under the same roof for months now, on the
closest terms of friendship, in a Mediterranean climate, with
the example of Neapolitan morals ever before them. Into
Nelson's mind had begun to creep the faint idea that the
ordinary laws of society did not apply to him, or it might be
better expressed by saying that this marvellous romance
which held him enthralled was not one of the vulgar
intrigues of which society rightly disapproved, but something of a far different quality, which he expected every one,
including his wife, to applaud and forward. He thought
Emma the most beautiful, the most talented, the most skilful woman the world had ever seen. The affection for Naples
with which she had earlier infected him was a most powerful

bond of sympathy which gave an idealist atmosphere to their relations. Their joint devotion to the Neapolitan Bourbons (which was hardly a result, at least on Nelson's side, of blind ignorance of their multiple failings) made a platform on which sordidness vanished.

Emma's experience had hardly been one which would develop rigid ideas of chastity. She had been betrayed by her first lover. She had been sold for a testamentary reward by the man to whom (it cannot be doubted) she gave all her young affections. Despite genuine efforts, she had never been able to cultivate a passion for courtly old Sir William with his artistic tastes and gentlemanly ineffectiveness. Fourteen years in southern Italy were not likely to give her a prejudice against marital unfaithfulness. Her passion for the limelight overmastered her. Sir William was old—he was seventy by now—and with his recall she would lose her position of dominance at Palermo. It is much to be doubted if she gave Nelson the affection she had once lavished on Greville. She treated him cavalierly enough in all conscience, gave him downright scoldings, while Nelson was never sure of her and was given to jealous fears. It seems likely that Emma was in love with the victor of the Nile rather than with Nelson, and with the Baron rather than with the Admiral.

Only one person's opinion of the business is doubtful, and that is Sir William's. There is no certainty as to whether he knew about it or not. Nelson believed he did not, but—there is room for doubt. Sir William must have been astonishingly blind if he did not see what the world saw. The blindness of husbands is proverbial; but in this case it was more pronounced than usual; it might have been deliberate. Sir William, with his yearning for peace, may have set Nelson the example of turning a blind eye to what he did not want to see. Certainly, except on the few occasions when Emma's feverish yearnings for excitement passed the bounds of his placid tolerance, he was besottedly fond of his wife and very much under her thumb. He neither wished to lose his wife nor to cause a colossal scandal. And he was very, very attached to Nelson too.

CHAPTER XII

TWO MONTHS IN ENGLAND

WHEN that fateful cruise ended at Palermo, it was to find that Nelson was given leave to go home (incidentally they heard that during the *Foudroyant*'s absence from Malta some small supplies reached Valetta by sea), while the King of Naples had become so thoroughly disgusted with his wife's handling of the business of the country, and had expressed himself with so much point, that the Queen had decided in tears to return for a time to her family in Vienna. So the *Foudroyant* sailed again to Leghorn, with Nelson, the Hamiltons, the Queen, thirty persons of the Royal suite, and various people attached to the Hamiltons on board.

At Leghorn the Queen hesitated between travelling overland, returning to Palermo, and going to Trieste by sea. Keith arrived, 'to be bored by Lord Nelson for permission to take the Queen to Palermo, and Princes and Princesses to all parts of the globe', so he wrote. He bluntly refused. He went so far as to say that Lady Hamilton had commanded the British Navy long enough. In the end they went by land, the Queen in floods of tears after a marked omission to bid Keith farewell, which did not trouble that worthy man in the least. The huge cortège trailed across Italy just in time to avoid the

French, who were pressing forward to reap the harvest of their victory at Marengo. The towns they traversed in the Papal States received them with enthusiasm. At Trieste, after their passage of the Adriatic, there were illuminations in Nelson's honour and crowds followed him in the street. At Vienna there were further demonstrations, and here they stayed for a month in consequence of Sir William's illness Then they said farewell to their 'dear Queen' and went on to Prague and Dresden.

But all was not well. People were talking. Lord Fitzharris described Emma as 'the most coarse, ill-mannered, disagreeable woman' he ever met. Her passion for gambling was readily remarked. At Dresden the Elector did not hold his Court during all their stay, in order to avoid having to invite them. Their stay there, however, was of advantage to history, because an English lady with a trenchant pen was staying there too, and made a series of illuminating though caustic criticisms of the party in her private journal. She notes the manner with which Emma 'puffed the incense full in Nelson's face', and how Nelson 'received it with pleasure'. She notes Sir William's submissiveness to and admiration for his wife, and describes the pitiable spectacle of this man of seventy 'hopping round the room on his backbone' for the entertainment of the party, ribbon and star flying. She notes Nelson's admiration for Emma, and his passionate devotion to the Queen of Naples. Although she was affected by the beauty of Emma's 'attitudes'—a series of classical poses which she often displayed for the entertainments of company—she still made note of Emma's liking for play and, worse, her tendency to heavy drinking. Altogether it is a pitiful picture which she presents of this odd trio roaming through Europe.

It was the 6th of November, 1800, that they reached Yarmouth, and the 9th before they came to London, after a triumphal progress through the Eastern counties. Nelson's leave had begun in May, so that he had not displayed extreme haste to meet his wife, whom he had left in March, 1798. For all that, he had no wish to separate from her. He had begun planning long before that he and Lady Nelson and the Hamiltons should set up house together; and Lady Nelson's refusal to approve of the scheme both shocked and surprised him. Lady Nelson had already formed suspicions as to the relations between the pair, apparently founded on rumours passed on by her son, Josiah. The manner of the arrival in England had annoyed her. She and Nelson's father had awaited Nelson in London; Lady Hamilton had ridden beside Nelson through the cheering crowds in Norwich. For two months Nelson strove to make the two women friends, and Lady Hamilton was quite agreeable; but Lady Nelson, while Mr Nelson remained a puzzled and hurt spectator, remained cold and aloof. Nelson invited the Hamiltons to dine at the lodgings he shared with his wife in Arlington Street; he made up parties of four for the theatre. But his method of endearing Lady Hamilton to Lady Nelson consisted in showing Emma the most lavish attention when he was with her, and in singing her praises every minute of the day when they were apart. Small wonder, then, that Lady Nelson one January morning announced that she was 'sick of hearing of dear Lady Hamilton', and, on Nelson's indignant expostulations, arising from table saying her mind was made up, and leaving the house with no more ado. She went to live once more with Nelson's father. Nelson had already seriously annoyed her by spending Christmas away from her in company with the Hamiltons at Fonthill Beckford.

The separation was by no means to Emma's taste. Her ambition was to be received at Court, and she soon found that she would have difficulty in achieving it. Society, and especially official society, was inclined to turn the cold shoulder to her. Quite apart from her parentage and her past, she could not be forgiven for the part she had played in the events in the Mediterranean. Keith's gibe that she had commanded the navy long enough found echoes elsewhere. She was not commanded to Court, and Nelson, her hot champion who was going round proclaiming her virtues, was coldly received there and at the Admiralty. Some elements of society, including Beckford of Fonthill, who thirsted for a peerage, were at first inclined to take them up, partly on account of the glamour of Nelson's victories and partly for the sake of the political influence Hamilton was believed to possess. But when Nelson began to live apart from his wife the scandal could not be ignored in the way Nelson had expected it to be. The King was a sincerely moral man, who turned resolute disapproval on such behaviour. Lady Hamilton began to be excluded from society. Moreover, the time had now come for her to make a voluntary, though temporary, retirement from society.

The event seems incredible, but in light of all the evidence now available it is hardly to be denied. Lady Hamilton was delivered of a child at Sir William's house, No 23 Piccadilly: The world did not know; Sir William did not know. She had appeared in public up to a month before. The plain-spoken and keenly observant Mrs St George had noticed nothing at Dresden in October, and the child was born at the end of January. But such a case is not without precedent. The lady who was either Countess of Bristol or Duchess of Kingston had a generation earlier been delivered of a child, unknown to the world, in the very precincts of the Court itself. As for Sir William, either he was too old, and too engrossed in his tangled affairs to notice anything, or else, as may be the case, he did not want to notice anything. Nelson and Lady Hamilton were exchanging letters which were intended to conceal the parentage of the child, and Sir William's letters to Nelson, which speak about his wife's indisposition, may have been directed to a similar aim. If they were, they were a good deal better planned than Nelson's (as might be expected of a professional diplomat), for Nelson's are contradictory and lapse into hopeless confusion between the delighted father, who was supposed to be on his ship, and himself, and between the delighted mother, who was supposed to be in Lady Hamilton's charge, and Lady Hamilton herself. Sir William, on the other hand, produced circumstantial and impressive evidence that his wife's indisposition proceeds 'from a foul stomach' and expresses simple delight at her recovery. His letters may yet have been sincere.

Nelson wrote various letters to Lady Hamilton. Some of them were intended for public display, as proof of parentage for the child, and these have always been available; but he wrote others which are more difficult to obtain, and have only recently become available, and these can leave no doubt whatever that Lady Hamilton bore a child of which he believed himself the father. Then all the arguments brought forward by the earlier biographers, who were not able to use this evidence, in denial of this fact, fall to the ground. All the same, it is barely possible that one part of Nelson's belief was unfounded. We have already alluded to one possible motive for his request for a knighthood instead of a baronetcy. And he had lived with Lady Nelson for years without children being born to them, although she had had a child by her first husband. The contention of Laughton and others that Horatia Nelson Thompson was not Nelson's daughter because her eyes were brown, while Emma's were blue and Nelson's grey, raises now only one other suspicion still less to

Emma's credit, seeing that the child was undoubtedly hers. And an opinion based on that suspicion is only opinion and nothing more. The writer's opinion is that the child was Nelson's, even while he is willing enough to admit that Lady Hamilton's passion for Nelson was not nearly as intense as his for her.

CHAPTER XIII

THE BALTIC

THE age-old question of the rights of neutrals was seemingly about to precipitate a terrible crisis in northern Europe. The tendency of a strong naval power to use (or in a neutral's eyes to abuse) her strength to the utmost was causing trouble; just as it had done in 1675, when France's insistence on the rights of blockade nearly made Charles II make war on Louis XIV, and in 1780, when the Armed Neutrality came into being, and as it was to do in 1916, when America had to choose between fighting England, who closed markets to her, and Germany, who killed her citizens.

Marengo and Hohenlinden had profoundly altered once more the balance of power in Europe. France was climbing to supremacy, and England's prestige was being correspondingly depressed, Sweden and Denmark had at first acquiesced, perforce, in England's restrictions on the profitableness of their neutrality. They had pocketed insults of various kinds, remaining at peace with England even after their ships of war had exchanged broadsides with English cruisers. But now France had conquered Austria again, and Russia, enraged at the Austrian treatment of Suvaroff, had withdrawn from the war, and fresh fuel was added daily to the fires of her resentment by the English treatment of Russian ships and merchandise. The imbecile King of

Denmark, the insane King of Sweden, and the unbalanced Czar of Russia began to draw closer together in a renewal of the armed neutrality of 1780, and to formulate demands which in English opinion would blunt the edge of England's only weapon, blockade. Lord Spencer at the Admiralty, and, after him, St Vincent, prevailed upon the tottering English Cabinet to adopt bold measures, and to strike hard at this embryo coalition, which could, if allowed time, back their demands with fifty ships of the line.

Vice-Admiral Lord Nelson, KB, had in January, 1801, hoisted his flag in the *San Josef* (his capture at St Vincent) in the Channel Fleet commanded by Lord St Vincent. Perhaps authority had decided that the iron-handed Jervis was the only man to control this restive subordinate. But the fall of Pitt's Government took St Vincent to the Admiralty, and the rapid development of the situation in the north called for bold action, and bold action called for the employment of Nelson, as he was available. He was transferred to Sir Hyde Parker's command, shifting his flag to the *St George*; he was at Yarmouth on the 6th of March.

Sir Hyde was a man of undistinguished record. As a young officer he had forced the entrance of North River during the American War of Independence—a feat which brought him his knighthood—and he had been Captain of the Fleet under Hood in the Mediterranean, but for some years since then he had vegetated as Governor of Jamaica. This was his first important naval command, and he seemed inclined to make the most of the moral perquisites of the appointment. There were junketings and festivities at Yarmouth, where Sir Hyde and his young wife held high revelry. He was not at all pleased by the nomination of Nelson as his second in command; he seems to have feared, and not unnaturally, that Nelson would wish to goad him into unpalatable activities in

which Parker would have all the responsibility and Nelson all
the glory. Parker treated Nelson with small consideration; he
was short with him at Nelson's official visit, and had no communication with him for days after that.

Nelson had no knowledge of the trend of the Admiralty
directions to Parker; officially, indeed, he did not know that
the Baltic was the objective of the expedition. All he knew
was that time was being frittered away, time which the
northern powers could employ with real profit in fortification
and preparation, time which might in the end melt the ice at
Reval and set free the Russian fleet to dispute the passage of
the Sound. He fretted and fumed at the waste of time; his
nerves were at the same time on the stretch with anxiety
about Lady Hamilton, whose child he had not yet seen, and
who was holding receptions in London again now which
were, significantly enough, attended mainly by men. He
wrote bitterly to Troubridge, now a Lord of the Admiralty,
about the delay, and later about Parker's extraordinary conduct in refusing him all information about the expedition.

The fleet sailed on March 12th, and some days later
Nelson still had not been taken into the confidence of the
Commander-in-Chief. The story runs that he eventually
contrived to gain Parker's confidence by the gift of a fine tur-
bot caught while passing the Dogger Bank, although this not
well-authenticated tale hardly agrees with Nelson's letters to
Troubridge. At any rate, during the fleet's slow progress to
the Skagerak Nelson at last succeeded in being called into
official consultation with Sir Hyde, and he began to deliver
reasoned appreciations and suggestions. Parker's Admiralty
orders indicated the likelihood of hostilities with Denmark,
Sweden and Russia, and laid down the need to subdue
Denmark before tackling the others. Nelson's first suggestion was to run past the Sound, and then first fall upon the

Russian squadron at Reval before it had a chance of aiding the Danes, or of being joined by the Petersburg squadron, which was still held idle by ice, or of taking refuge behind the batteries of Kronstadt. Parker set this aside, possibly from fear that the Danish ships might escape to France— which was not very likely—or on account of a Commander-in-Chief's natural aversion to fighting a pitched battle with an enemy across his rear. Nelson's other suggestion, and one which was later adopted with minor modifications, was to pass the Sound, thus gaining an interior position, and then to attack Copenhagen. What Nelson laid particular stress upon was the need not to begin negotiations until an overwhelming force was at hand ready for instant attack. A year before nine ships of the line had sufficed to intimidate the Danes, but that was before Russia was a probable Danish ally—the important argument in favour of the suggested blow against Reval. This time the Danes were supported by the hope of Russian assistance and, warned by previous experience, had done much to establish defences for their capital, although, having, as was only natural, left much of the work until the need was urgent, much that remained to be done was still only in process of arrangement.

Yet delays occurred. On March 20th the English envoy was landed to deliver the ultimatum, and he did not return until the 23rd with the news of its rejection, during which time the fleet remained at anchor in the Kattegat. He brought back information as to the strength of the defences, which alarmed Parker, and made him hark back to his original plan of waiting outside the Baltic until the hostile powers had mustered their strength to come out and fight him—a plan which would leave on England's hands another blockade under difficult conditions, and a steadily growing enemy, and which would mean probably the closing of the Baltic to

English shipping until the end of the war. Parker, however, called a council, and thereat was persuaded by Nelson to enter the Baltic and risk a blow at Copenhagen. There was further delay caused by Parker's indecision as to whether to go by the Belt or the Sound, and by adverse weather conditions after he changed his mind—poor man, he felt extremely the burden of doubt as to what attitude Sweden with her mad King and faction-torn aristocracy would adopt—but at last, on the 30th March, the ships ran through into the Sound. The Swedish batteries did not open, and the ships, keeping over to the Swedish side, were out of range of the Danish batteries.

The same day Parker and Nelson reconnoitred the Danish defences. Parker and many of the senior officers were impressed by them, but Nelson, admitting that they looked 'formidable to those who are children at war', announced that with ten sail of the line he thought he could fall upon them from their weaker interior end and destroy them, so that the bomb vessels could get into range of the city and threaten its destruction. Parker at length gave him leave to try. He was not very hopeful, seemingly expecting another Santa Cruz disaster, and being possessed with fears of being attacked by the Russian and Swedish fleets with half his ships crippled; but Nelson, who displayed extreme contempt for the fighting value of these potential enemies (which was certainly well-founded), carried him away by the force and fire of his personality.

Twelve of the lightest ships of the line (Nelson had transferred his flag to the *Elephant*, 74, Captain Foley) and all the small craft were allotted to Nelson. The channel was rebuoyed, soundings were taken, and the batteries reconnoitred as well as might be. On April 1st they took advantage of the westerly wind to run down the northern channel and to moor at the southern end of the shoal which lay between that passage and the King's Channel, where the batteries were. Then all that remained to do was to issue the orders for the attack, and to wait for an easterly wind which would carry them back up the King's Channel against the weaker end of the long line of defences.

It was an exciting night, for delay meant not merely the further strengthening of the Danish defences, but actual danger from shells if the Danes brought up sufficient mortars into range of the mooring, as they could do. Nelson dictated his orders—as it grew late he continued them from his cot—with reports still coming in. The orders were given to the clerks to transcribe at one in the morning, but Nelson could not sleep. He was too anxious about the wind, and, sure enough, his previous promptitude was rewarded by the wind shifting into the east. Had he delayed his advance one more day, that east wind would have kept him from reaching his present mooring; he would have had to wait for a westerly wind and then again for an easterly one—days of waiting, perhaps.

At seven o'clock all the captains were on board the *Elephant*, and a last conference, reminiscent of those which preceded the Nile, was held. At eight o'clock the attack was ordered, and a new difficulty arose, for the pilots, eyeing the long line of Danish batteries with apprehension, shrank from the task of taking ships of the line, of deep draught and not amenable to delicate handling, up the difficult King's Channel. One pilot was at last coerced into his duty, and the ships weighed anchor in succession. The *Agamemnon* could not weather the central shoal, and so never came into action. The *Bellona* and the *Russell*, keeping too far from the batteries, ran on the shoal, but were able to use their guns at long range. The other nine came into action in succession against the weak southern end of the defences, concentrating their attack upon it as they filed past.

Here there were seven small mastless ships of the line, anchored on the Danish edge of the channel, with eleven smaller floating batteries. North of them was the powerful Trekroner battery, on land, and beyond that two more large hulks. Nelson's attack was confined to the hulks south of the Trekroner; the frigates and small craft under Captain Riou flung themselves against the remainder —assuming the duty allotted by Nelson's orders to the ships aground—and were roughly handled, Riou being killed, although they did serious damage before they retired.

As the English ships came up, they were met by a tremendous artillery fire, the Danes using their guns better than Nelson had expected. But there was nothing on earth comparable with the fire of English guns served by English seamen. The Danish vessels were shattered terribly by the English fire. Nelson, pressing into action behind the leaders, made for the position beside the Danish flagship vacant through the *Bellona*'s absence. He wanted to be close alongside, but with the water shoaling down to four fathoms, the pilots and the master lost their nerve and the *Elephant* anchored two hundred yards away, when actually the water deepened right up to the Danish line.

Each ship as she came up anchored by the stern in position opposing the hulks; the absence of the two ships aground and of *Agamemnon* caused no confusion. The fire was intense, and Nelson, walking the quarter-deck of the *Elephant* with Foley and Colonel Stewart, made his oft-quoted remark that he 'would not be elsewhere for thousands'. Meanwhile Parker with the heavier ships was beating up against the easterly wind to give the aid which he had promised to give if he could, but it was hard to work to windward in such a narrow and tricky channel. He could do nothing to help, and he could see nothing. He flew the signal for recall, to which Nelson turned his blind eye, providing a new metaphor for the English language and a new tradition for the English fleet.

Riou obeyed the signal, meeting his death-wound as he turned his ship's stern to the raking fire of the Trekroner. Nelson refused to repeat the signal, and his ships continued the battle. The event proved Nelson right; but in any case it was not a very wise action on Parker's part to interfere in a battle with floating batteries when he was four miles off and had in consequence no means of telling what damage had been done to the enemy, not even the fall of masts. It is, in consequence partly of this fact that it has been argued that there was an agreement between Nelson and Parker by which the latter was to hoist the signal and take the responsibility, while the former could obey or not as his judgment dictated. Parker, indeed, after a worried conference with his Captain of the Fleet and Otway, his Flag-Captain, sent Otway to try and ascertain what was happening, but before he reached the *Elephant* Parker's fears overcame him and he had the signal hoisted. It can hardly be thought that Nelson would have been as agitated about his disobedience as he was, if there had been any previous agreement; still less is it likely that Nelson would later have taken the credit for his action without explanation, nor Parker to have allowed him to do so without protest.

Soon afterwards the Danish fire began to slacken. Some of their floating batteries were on fire, some had drifted out of position through the cutting of their cables by shot, and all had suffered tremendous loss of men, which, although it was numerically made good in part by reinforcements ferried out from the shore, affected the rate of fire and accuracy of aim by reason of the lack of training of the newcomers. Some of the shattered batteries drifted under the fire of the Trekroner, where they were raked both by friend and foe. Colours were shot away and were not replaced, so that the English believed that surrendered vessels had reopened fire. Wounded men burned to death because of the fire which was directed on the boats of the rescuing Englishmen. At last, while a spasmodic fire was still maintained on the Danish side, Nelson sent on shore a flag of truce demanding cessation of fire, pointing out that unless it was granted he would have to burn the captured floating batteries without having time to rescue the wounded on board. The Danes sent back asking for a more explicit message, and as the Crown Prince's aide-de-camp, who bore the request, was willing to discuss terms for a definite armistice he was sent on to Parker, while Nelson expanded his first message into a suggestion that hostilities should cease while he secured his prisoners and prizes, and sent the wounded on shore. Before this second message was landed, however, the Crown Prince had given orders to cease firing, flags of truce were raised, and Nelson proceeded to take away his own ships and those of the prizes fit to move. For this he has been accused of sharp practice, but clearly there was none. He made no promise, nor suggested one, although it cannot be denied (it has no relation to the argument) that his ships were very seriously damaged—far more so than at the Nile—and the sooner some of them were got out of harm's way from shoals and batteries the better, especially as with the easterly wind the only way open to junction with Parker lay under the guns of the unsubdued Trekroner.

But the battle was won. There was now nothing to prevent the British mortar vessels from moving into range and bombarding the town, the docks and the shipping, and under threat of this action the Copenhagen Government must make peace. The very next day Parker sent Nelson into the town to open negotiations with the Crown Prince. Nelson himself was still vehemently in favour of a move upon Reval, arguing correctly that defeat of the Russians would make the Danes more conscious of their weakness, besides soothing the smart of their injured national pride and relieving them of an ever-present menace. But Parker would not stir until he was sure of Denmark's attitude, so that day after day Nelson appeared in Copenhagen, guarded from the half-curious, half-hostile crowd, to wring at least benevolent neutrality out of the sullen Danes. It was a difficult business. Nelson had only one card to play, although it was the most powerful in the pack: that was the bombardment of the city. The English could ruin the port and the buildings of Copenhagen, but, if they were forced to do that, the Danes would be driven to desperation, while the fleet could do no more. They had not sufficient troops to subjugate the country—a want which was provided for in 1807—and Parker would not in that case penetrate farther into the Baltic. But Nelson used the threat to the utmost of its value.

Suddenly the news came that even before the battle the Czar Paul had met his death in a palace revolution. From what was known of his successor further Russian hostility to England was unlikely, and the Danes yielded. An armistice for fourteen weeks was agreed upon, during which Denmark was to withdraw from the Armed Neutrality, make no attempt to rearm, and to open her ports to the English fleet. In return the English only promised immunity for the Danish coasts—Norway, Holstein and the colonies were all left open to English attack. It was a marvellous good bargain, and one of which Nelson was justifiably proud; he was not unnaturally nettled by the cautious reply from London that 'upon a consideration of all the circumstances, His Majesty has thought fit to approve'.

Indeed, the attitude of the Government towards the victors of Copenhagen irritated Nelson profoundly to the end of his days. He himself received a step in the peerage, becoming Viscount Nelson, with remainder of his barony to his father's descendants, while Graves, the Rear-Admiral with Nelson, was given the Order of the Bath; but his other officers and men were given no distinction, and there was no vote of thanks by Parliament to the active squadron, nor by the Common Council—no public recognition of any sort. This was probably due to the dislike of the Government to calling attention to the victory after peace with Denmark, although it may also have been due to the Admiralty's shrinking from the invidious business of having to differentiate between Nelson and Parker, between the Captains who fought and those who were left out. If this was so, it was a grave error on the part of St Vincent and Troubridge. Later the City of London's neglect was to call forth a cold refusal from Nelson to the Lord Mayor of London's invitation to the public dinner, and he was more than once to declare that his acceptance could only be purchased by the gift to Graves of the Freedom of the City in a gold box.

At last Parker decided to move into the Baltic. The ships passed the shoals by transferring their guns to merchant vessels, although the *St George*, being delayed, was left behind for a time with Nelson fuming and fretting on board, for an interval during which, on the receipt of a rumour that the Swedish fleet was coming out for battle, he had himself rowed twenty-four miles in a small boat on a cold night to the main body. Parker dallied for a time in the Baltic, and then, refusing to take up a station off Reval which would place him in position to intercept the squadron there, that at

Kronstadt, and that at Karlskrona, he went feebly back to
Kioge Bay beside Copenhagen. Eventually, when it was too
late, Parker was recalled and Nelson became Commander-in-
Chief—another cause of irritation, not one of satisfaction.

His first order was to weigh anchor, and sail was set for
Reval, but by now the ice was gone, and with it the Russian
squadron, which lay safe at last under the guns of Kronstadt.
So that now his appearance only exposed him to a sharp
snub, and it took all Nelson's tactful haughtiness to extricate
him from the difficult position in which his predecessor's
dilatoriness had placed him. There was nothing for a Nelson
to do now in the Baltic.

Moreover, he had been exposed to many other sources of
worry. The Commander-in-Chief of the Danish fleet had
written publicly condemning Nelson's action with the flag of
truce at Copenhagen as sharp practice or worse, and Nelson
became involved in a paper controversy with him which was
not softened by the fact that the Dane had not been conspicuous for personal courage in the battle, twice shifting his
flag, the first time from a vessel which fought on until the
end of the battle and the second time to the comparative
safety of the Trekroner. But there were terrible troubles
beside which this petty argument was but a pin-prick. There
had been a letter sent to Davison, the strange man who
acted as Nelson's agent, who was supposed to have saved
Nelson from marriage at Quebec, navy agent, banker, com-
missariat contractor, Commissary-General of the Forces and
Treasurer of the Ordnance, unseated member of Parliament,
who had seen the inside of a prison once and was to do so
again, but who remained throughout Nelson's confidant and
best adviser. This letter directed Davison to inform 'Lady N'
before Nelson's return to England that he expected 'to be
left to himself and without any inquiries from her'. The poor

woman was to be flung out of Nelson's life as dispassionately as she was brought into it.

Ever since Nelson had rehoisted his flag letters had been coming in from Lady Hamilton, letters which he himself destroyed, but whose purport we can deduce from the pitiful replies which are now open to our examination. She had displayed fierce jealousy towards Lady Nelson, ascertaining her movements lest she should be trying to close the gap between them, and madly accusing Nelson of writing to her, an accusation which Nelson could only pitifully answer by the declaration that he had never written to 'his aunt' (so the pair alluded to Lady Nelson) except letters which Lady Hamilton knew all about. Not only that, but Emma went on to accuse him of meditated unfaithfulness to her on all sorts of occasions, basing one attack of this sort on a casual reference of Nelson's to the fact that West-countrywomen wore black stockings. To each accusation Nelson sent only timid denials, protesting against such attacks, bearing with her mad jealousy in a manner that contrasts unpleasantly with his hot replies, written on the same days, to Commodore Fischer's insinuations. To pacify her jealousy he was willing to make any sacrifice; Lady Nelson was finally dismissed, and he never set foot on land save when his duty commanded it.

Moreover, letters both from Lady Hamilton and from others were driving him, too, nearly distraught with jealousy. The Prince of Wales was calling upon the Hamiltons, and it seemed to Nelson that Sir William would sell Emma to him as willingly as Greville had sold her to Sir William. The Prince's reputation was well known and Nelson raved against him in his letters far more vehemently than ever he wrote about the hated French. He raved and he raged impotently. He knew the King was mad, and that if a Regency were

arranged the Prince's word would do much to establish a
Royal dockyard at Milford Haven in the heart of Sir William's
developing estates. Nelson's letters give the impression that
he was maddened by fear. They wring the heart—'but for-
give me, I know my Emma, and don't forget you had once a
Nelson, a friend, a dear friend, but, alas! he has his misfor-
tunes. He has lost his best friend, his only friend, his only
love. Don't forget him, poor fellow'. He is calmer at other
times, and assures his precious friend that his constancy is
such that he could be trusted in a dark room full of naked vir-
gins. Yet the worry was constant; there were others besides
the Prince, and Nelson, who knew of the favours enjoyed in
turn by Greville, whom he calls 'that other', by Sir William,
and by himself (even if he knew not of Greville's predeces-
sors) was terrified in case he was not to be the last of the list.

Worried by all these fears, made ill by the climate (at least,
it was that to which he attributed his prostration), annoyed
by his appointment to the command too late to achieve anything, he began to write pressingly for his recall. It was
granted. Vice-Admiral Cole came out to relieve him; on June
19th he set sail on his return, and on July 1st he reached
Yarmouth.

CHAPTER XIV

THE CHANNEL AND MERTON

O VER the England to which he returned had fallen the shadow of a new menace. Bonaparte had forced peace upon Austria, had made friends with Russia, had kept Prussia neutral, so that once more France was left without a continental enemy to occupy her attention. Along the North Sea coast of Flanders, along the Channel coasts of France, preparations were being made for an invasion of England. There were French troops ready in numbers far superior to any English regular army which could oppose them. There were flotillas of flat boats built and building to carry them over. The nervous apprehensions of the English public magnified a real danger into an imminent catastrophe. The Admiralty had kept its head. To oppose the flotilla it kept ready such a force of frigates and smaller vessels, backed by a few ships of the line, that any chance of the flotilla crossing without damage was nearly negligible as long as it had not battleship support; and battleship support was denied it by the blockade of the French Biscay and Mediterranean ports which was resolutely maintained in face of all difficulties. Even if an army were hastily ferried out in a calm, a fog, darkness or other weather conditions which kept the sailing ships out of

action, there were light gunboats in plenty to oppose the
crossing, and it seemed unlikely that the troops could be got
on board quickly enough or could row rapidly enough to take
advantage of such conditions while they lasted. And all this
left undiscussed the question as to whether a French army,
devoid of communications, and equipped only with what the
flat boats could carry, would be able to do much harm if by a
combination of improbabilities it succeeded in landing.

But the British public was not appreciative of these considerations. It was nervous about invasion; even the Cabinet
was unsettled in its mind, just as in August, 1914, troops
were held back for fear of a landing against which the
Admiralty gave, at the time, the fullest possible guarantee.
To reassure the public and to quiet the general restlessness
the Government appealed to Nelson. He was the man who
had captured one ship across the deck of another, who had
destroyed the French at the Nile, who had beaten the Danes
at Copenhagen. The knowledge that he was in command in
the narrow seas would comfort the English mind.

Nelson was not particularly pleased with the request. He
was longing for peace and retirement and the continued
society of Emma Hamilton. He had returned from the Baltic
with the desire to seclude himself with her at Bronté, where
Princes of Wales were not likely to come; but Emma had
shown a surprising reluctance to shut herself up in a tumble-
down farmhouse in Sicily, forty miles from a carriage road.
The devoted trio, Nelson, Emma and Sir William, had gone
to Staines for a holiday immediately upon Nelson's arrival in
England, and at Staines Emma succeeded in convincing him
that nothing on earth would induce her to go into retirement
with him anywhere on earth. A kind of compromise was
decided upon. Nelson was to buy an estate not too far from
London, and the Hamiltons were to share it with him.

Apparently Nelson believed that here he would find the rest and solitude for which he yearned; Sir William was cozened into the belief that here he too would enjoy the mild intellectual pleasures his declining years demanded. Lady Hamilton's plans, not readily disclosed, did not give much countenance to either hope. Meanwhile St Vincent was pressing Nelson to accept the command offered him, and writing in a very serious vein to beg him not to throw away the career of brilliance which was opening before him and upon which he had made so headlong a start. After three weeks at Staines Nelson yielded. Perhaps St Vincent's solicitations were effective; perhaps Emma's indignant refusal to share a cottage had something to do with it; perhaps Emma may have urged him into acceptance (it seems very likely), because Nelson, forgotten by the public, would be of no use to her whatever. Sir William went off to Wales to see what he could do towards settling the dreadful muddle Greville had made of the management of the Pembroke estates. Lady Hamilton came to London to look for estates just outside the suburbs, at Merton, Turnham Green and elsewhere. Nelson hoisted his flag in *L'Unité* frigate, at Sheerness.

He had already submitted to the Admiralty his amazing memorandum on the problem of defence against invasion. His grasp of most of the essentials of the business was bold and unhesitating. His appreciation of the advantages and the disadvantages of the French position was perfectly clear, and although he made no suggestions improving greatly on the plans already developed, he brought all his energy and force of personality into the task of making the most of the means at hand. But what was surprising was his firm conviction that the French would divide their forces; that they would despatch one flotilla from Dunkirk and the neighbourhood and another from Boulogne, simultaneously but quite separately, and would continue the system, having landed, by advancing on London with two columns of twenty thousand men each, divided by a considerable interval. Nothing can appear more certain than that the French would have done nothing of the sort. Of necessity their flotillas would have started separately, because of the smallness of the harbours, but even against unmilitary England it seems unlikely that they would not have done all they could to unite their forces at the earliest possible moment. The military strength of England could be relied upon to defeat twenty thousand men; even forty thousand would not find their task too easy. Nelson here, as in several other cases, was not displaying good judgment on the employment of large military forces.

The command assigned to him ran from Orfordness to Beachy Head, and was carved out of those held by various other Admirals, whose natural objections to this modified supercession were tactfully disposed of by St Vincent and by Nelson. The new commander threw himself with energy into his task, even though it might not have been with good-will. He was not a firm believer in the danger of invasion, and the work was distasteful to him for the very practical reason that it meant constant living in small vessels in rough water, with the result that he was continually seasick and much inconvenienced, because of the loss of his arm, by the extravagant motion of the vessels. Boarding and leaving his ship were now undignified and difficult proceedings because of his crippled condition. And of course active service meant separation from Emma.

But he did his duty manfully, drumming up the Sea Fencibles who were supposed to be ready to volunteer in the event of invasion, reconnoitring the French ports, and soon beginning to annoy the shipping there by shelling it from mortar vessels. He was accompanied by a young officer,

Captain Parker, whose acquaintance he had made in the Baltic, for whom he cherished a great affection, and whose talents he was continually praising. A fortnight after his arrival in the Channel he launched a serious attack on a French flotilla moored outside the harbour of Boulogne. It was made from boats, and by night, and it was unsuccessful. In the darkness the various divisions moving to the attack lost touch, and came separately into action. Parker, arriving first, was shot through the thigh and was beaten back by the French, who were on their guard. The other detachments were roughly handled on their arrival, and the whole attempt ended only in loss and irritation. Yet next day he was cheerfully writing that he had 'real thoughts of attacking the enemy at Flushing'; but careful reconnaissance outside that port convinced him that the approaches were too difficult and the defence was too strong.

There was some murmuring in the fleet about the waste of life at Boulogne, and it was re-echoed on land; for a little it seemed as if Nelson's popularity, one of his sources of strength, was imperilled, but the murmurs died down before long. Quite soon Nelson came to the conclusion that he could effect little against the enemy's coasts, while at the same time he grew convinced that there was no possibility of invasion being attempted without battleship support, and the public inclined to his point of view, much to the increase of its peace of mind. He, however, was ill at ease both mentally and physically, and he began once more to hanker after retirement, sending in requests for leave which were refused by the Admiralty. It is to be suspected that St Vincent and Troubridge were planning to keep him away from Lady Hamilton, and despite his complaints they maintained him in his command in his little flagship as she pitched at her anchors. He was tormented with sea-sickness, toothache, neuralgia, as well as the vaguer troubles to which he continually described himself as subject. For a space he was happy, when Sir William, as obliging as ever, brought Lady Hamilton down to Deal for a fortnight. Nelson had champagne sent down from London for their entertainment; he himself kept nothing of the kind to offer them, and he knew it would be wanted. Emma was beginning that habit of hard drinking which, together with her passion for gambling, was to ruin her.

But in September, after the Hamiltons had departed again, depression seized upon him harder than ever. Young Parker died of his wounds, to Nelson's bitter sorrow—'I beg that his hair may be cut off and given to me; it shall remain and be buried with me'—and there were libellous attacks made upon his conduct in command. Eventually, after a weary wait, the Peace of Amiens was signed, and he was able to gain his heart's desire, and bury himself in what Lady Hamilton had written to describe as the 'Paradise' of Merton.

She and Sir William had bought the place and furnished it with money supplied by Nelson, and, seemingly, drove a good bargain. Nelson was delighted with what he found there on his arrival in October, 1801, and he looked forward to long happiness at Merton. But happiness is elusive. Sir William was rather a nuisance. Nelson disliked him only for what he stood for, not for what he was, but the dislike made itself evident. Nelson did not like the idea of Emma having a husband, even one as complaisant and unexacting as Sir William. It was on this account that he harked back occasionally to the old scheme of going off to Bronté, leaving Sir William behind, but Emma refused steadfastly. Sir William's presence at Merton made their mode of life together apparently respectable, and Emma still clung passionately to what few shreds of respectability remained to her.

And Sir William was not too happy. He was worried about money—Greville's Milford Haven schemes had dredged his purse and forced him to live upon the realization of investments. Emma insisted on the maintenance of their Piccadilly house, although they were living permanently at Merton, and she was housekeeping in a style of extravagance (Hamilton and Nelson were sharing expenses) which caused him some anxiety. It was irksome, too, 'to have seldom less than twelve or fourteen at table', and such festivities interfered sadly with his attendance at 'the Museum, the Royal Society, the Tuesday Club, and Auctions of Pictures', and his 'fishing parties on the Thames'. He wanted 'no more silly altercations', and rather than suffer a continuance of them he would insist on a 'wise and well-concerted separation'. He even, in the letter from which the quotations are drawn, ventured to hint that 'the whole attention of his wife was given to Lord N', although he hastened to declare his certainty of the 'purity of Lord N's friendship'.

Lady Hamilton was the only one of the trio whose plans were being fulfilled, and even she felt none too comfortable. She had abandoned her attempt to enter Court circles—Sir William made occasional appearances therein without her—but was instead turning towards the faster set, which she entertained with much display and luxury at Merton. In these entertainments she satisfied her urgent need for lavishness, and could dull the regret that she was not a Lady-in-Waiting and that the ladies were not half as anxious to call on her as the gentlemen were. Sir William's threat to separate from her frightened her—it would be as bad as her leaving him to go to Bronté in Nelson's company—and, furthermore, she was scheming to oust Greville from his will. She exerted herself to mollify him after this very rare outburst.

Nelson's relations were frequent visitors at Merton. His brothers, his sisters and his father came there. He had made presents to all of them, and he made money allowances to his sisters for their children's education, while, as already noted, Mr Nelson received (or should have received, if the estate produced that much) £500 a year from Bronté. It is hard to discover what all these people thought about the Nelson-Hamilton affair. His father seemingly never knew the truth; the others may have been too fascinated by their splendid brother to believe it, or perhaps they pocketed their scruples. Certain it is that Nelson's brother, Maurice, lived for years with a woman to whom he was not married, and upon his death, in 1802, Nelson made her an allowance which he confirmed as an annuity in his will. But later it is equally certain that the survivors of the Nelson family turned away from Lady Hamilton—after Nelson's death—with speed.

Most of the callers were men with whom Nelson had come into contact in the course of his professional career—Lord Minto, Lord Hood (who presented Nelson when he took his seat in the House of Lords as a Viscount), Ball, Saumarez, Troubridge. They found there a very quiet gentleman in a black suit, toothless, yellow, shrunken, the very soul of hospitality and politeness, whom they had once known as the fiercest and most brilliant sailor in the whole Navy. He deferred to a very tall woman, immensely stout, with a ravaged complexion, coarse in manner and beginning to be coarse in appearance, with a tendency to drink more champagne than was quite seemly, and whose one wish after leaving the dinner table was to settle down to cards. Somewhere in the background there was a vague shadow of a man, elegant of dress and deportment, despite the fact that his back was bent and his step tottering with years, who seemed to spend his time looking after the lady's lapdogs and footstool, and who, if anyone condescended to enter into conversation with him, would confess to a taste for quiet fishing which he unfortunately had little chance of indulging.

In the summer of 1802 the quaint trio went off once more on a journey across England; that Milford Haven property of Sir William's was clamouring for attention. They went by way of Dorking to Oxford (where, at Blenheim, the Duke of Marlborough avoided the honour of receiving them in person), and so through Gloucester to Swansea. Most places gave them a great reception, with ringing of bells and presenting of addresses, although some of the wealthier people disliked Lady Hamilton both by reputation and at first sight. The poorer folk either did not know of the circumstances which united the trio or (as seems likely) did not care. Nelson described the way he had been received as 'most flattering to my feelings'—although in the same letter he gave vent to the bitterness of his mind caused by comparison of this treatment with that offered by persons in high places. The refusal of the Court to notice his Emma's existence still rankled; so did the fact that the Nile and Copenhagen between them had only added £1000 a year to his pension, as compared with the £3000 given for Camperdown and St Vincent.

Time went on. Nelson was leading, for him, an idle life. He submitted a few memoranda to the Admiralty, on the conservation of the supplies of British oak, and on the prevention of desertion among seamen of the navy (both problems which greatly exercised the minds of naval officers at that time), and he spoke once or twice in the House of Lords—most notably on an ominous occasion when Napoleon's violations of the spirit of the Peace of Amiens caused a wave of uneasiness in the mind of the Government. His father had died in 1802. In April, 1803, there was another death, which had a profounder influence on Nelson's career.

Poor old Sir William had managed to struggle through the winter, but at last, worn out by his seventy-two years, by the money quarrels with his wife (which had continued), by the exertions she demanded of him, by his worry about his property, and perhaps by his worry about Nelson, he had died 'without a struggle' in Nelson's and Lady Hamilton's arms. His will left to his widow a few hundred pounds in cash and an annuity of £800, a reasonable enough amount, but one which Sir William must have known would be a mere drop in the ocean of her spendings. To Nelson he left a portrait of his wife, alluding to him as 'the most virtuous, loyal, and truly brave character I have ever met with'. But he went on to recognize the possibility of the existence of some who might not say 'Amen' to Sir William's 'God bless him'. All the rest of the property went to Greville, who now at last received his reward for his self-denial in sending Emma to Naples seventeen years before.

But the fact that Sir William had survived the winter of 1802–3 was of great importance. It was Sir William who had constituted the main obstacle to the realization of Nelson's scheme of retirement to Bronté. While he was alive there could be no scandal obvious to those who had not the evidence of their eyes, and Nelson was retained where he would still be useful to his country should the need arise. The need had by now arisen.

CHAPTER XV

THE BLOCKADE

IMMEDIATELY after the Peace of Amiens had been signed every one came to realize that it was only a truce. In addition to the instinctive hostility of the English ruling class to the French system of government there was the French domination of Lombardy, Tuscany and Genoa, the French army of occupation in southern Italy, and the rapid regeneration of the French Navy to create distrust. With French dominion over the shores of the Mediterranean being so rapidly extended and confirmed, England had to retain Malta lest she should be driven altogether from that sea. It was a vicious circle of mutual irritation, culminating on May 16th, 1803, in a British declaration of war.

Nelson had already been warned, on May 6th, that his services might be required; on the 16th he was given the Mediterranean command, with orders to hoist his flag in the ship whose name will always be associated with his, but which had already flown the flag of Hood and Jervis and half a score of famous Admirals before them. For one little month he had been at Merton with his Emma, without Sir William's kindly chaperonage, but the interval had been so short and the times so exacting that the circumstances had escaped public comment. He had busied himself in the interval with the hopeless task of ensuring Lady Hamilton's financial sta-

bility. He allowed her £1200 a year from his own resources—
his income only amounted to £4000, of which he paid Lady
Nelson £1800, and to other dependents £350. He had
pestered, at Emma's request, a great many people in support
of her demand for a pension—a pension which, oddly
enough, might have been granted if only she would admit
that she was his mistress. He gave her Merton to live in, and
she promptly took another house in Clarges Street as well.
With two thousand a year and Merton anyone might expect
her to be well off, even Nelson, who should have known her
so well.

As far as is known, Lady Hamilton did nothing to hold him
back from his duty, and all circumstantial evidence goes to
point to the contrary. She was, indeed, by no means as fond
of him as he of her, and it seems that she saw him go without regret, and turned again instantly to what society she
could find in London—the horrid old Duke of Queensberry
was one of her acquaintances—to a life of hectic excitement
(the recent death of her husband notwithstanding) and of
rapid accumulation of debt. Only after Nelson had been
gone for two years did she begin to have fears that his affection for her might wane as had his affection for Fanny
Nelson.

Nelson himself was glad to go; idleness had become a
curse, and it is to be suspected that he felt a yearning for the
ordered routine of shipboard life and the unchallenged position of a Commander-in-Chief after the late hours and melo-
dramatic jealousies of Merton. On May 18th he hoisted his
flag on board the *Victory* at Portsmouth, and on the 20th he
sailed—fuming at the intervening delay. His orders were to
the effect that after his arrival in the Mediterranean he was
to look to the safety of Malta, to do what could be done
about the destruction of the French fleet at Toulon, to be

ready to protect Naples, Egypt and Corfu against French attack, to keep a careful eye upon naval preparations in Spanish ports as far round as Cadiz, to be ready to prevent a junction of French, Spanish and Dutch ships, to protect Neapolitan and Turkish commerce as well as English, to intercept French ships of the line which were expected from the West Indies, and to keep watch upon French proceedings in Genoa, Leghorn and other Italian ports. His duties bade fair to be in sharp contrast with the idleness of Merton.

On his way out he was to find if Cornwallis, commanding the squadron off Brest, needed temporarily the services of the *Victory*, and in that case Cornwallis was to have her. Cornwallis was not on the rendezvous; there was no finding him either at sea or close in to the land. Twenty-four hours' delay was enough for Nelson. He left the *Victory* to continue the search, bundled himself and his staff into the frigate *Amphion*—'seven or eight in one cabin', he wrote—and dashed on. Less than a day at Gibraltar sufficed for the issue of orders for the state of war, news of which the *Amphion* was the first to bring, and on June 15th Nelson was at Malta. There he plunged into the business of doing what could be done to secure Naples and Sicily from the French. His orders were sent out, and, thirty-six hours after his arrival, he left again in search of Sir Richard Bickerton and the fleet, which was off Toulon. It took three weeks to get there, an experience which prejudiced Nelson against Malta from the first; indeed, the island was not extremely useful as a base for a sailing fleet operating against an enemy in Toulon, and its true value only became apparent in the days of steam with the opening of the Suez Canal.

But it was a solid base, impregnable with its English garrison to any flying attack that the French might deliver, and as such it was of extreme value until Nelson had worked out a

system by which Sardinian shelter could be employed. Sicily
was far more open to attack. The French could have Naples
for the taking, and, once established there, it was quite likely
that they could ferry a body of troops across the Straits of
Messina. There were no illusions now about the value of the
Sicilian troops, nor about the loyalty to the Bourbons of the
Sicilian people. Nelson began to press for the transfer of
English troops to Messina; the Neapolitan Government
began its usual shifty tactics. An English army at Messina
would be a proof of the breach of Neapolitan neutrality, and
in that case Naples would fall to the French, a disaster which
must be postponed as long as possible, even if postponement
meant risking the loss of Sicily as well. It was a nice point to
decide, especially as there were already thirteen thousand
French soldiers in Apulia, holding the heel of Italy and ready
for transference either to Corfu or to Naples as need or
opportunity arose. The situation occupied much of Nelson's
attention, and the strength of the French garrisons of
Brindisi and Otranto necessitated placing the greater part of
Nelson's woefully few frigates round the exit to the Adriatic.

He had to watch the fluctuations of the political world
with extreme care. A Franco-Russian alliance, which was still
possible, might mean a joint attack upon Turkey and the
sending of French agents and detachments to raise rebellion
in Greece; it would certainly mean difficulties for the central
command. The attitude of Spain was more menacing. It was
known that by treaty Spain was paying France an annual sub-
sidy; at any moment Napoleon might decide that Spanish
ships were of more use to him than Spanish gold, and the
entry of Spain into the war would mean severe pressure on
Nelson's communications from the Spanish fleet, further
raids on British commerce by privateers, the closing of the
already not-too-hospitable Spanish ports to British ships,

and the cessation of the meagre but invaluable supply of
fresh provisions which he drew from Catalonia. The States of
the Church were in a more dangerous position even than
Naples. Nominally neutral, they were being traversed and
re-traversed by French armies to which His Holiness could
offer no opposition whatever. At any moment they might be
driven into war with England, and Nelson foresaw that this
would happen the moment the French found that he was
drawing any advantage whatever from their neutrality.
Tuscany and Genoa were quite subject to the French, and
their ports were convenient places of call for Austrian and
Greek ships, where cargo might be transferred to coasting
vessels for the supply of southern France, just as they had
been all the other times that Nelson had served in the
Mediterranean. Nelson's instant recommendation, which
was approved, was the blockade of this coast. Sardinia, ruled
by the most timid and nearly the most unfortunate representative of the House of Savoy, was striving to maintain a
neutrality which would satisfy the French. Piedmont, the
most valuable part of the kingdom, was now part of France,
but the Sardinian King bore with that lest worse befall him;
invasion of Sardinia from Corsica seemed easy enough, and
he feared lest he might be stripped even of this last poor
fragment of territory. The result was that at first he refused
to British ships even the limited hospitality usual in neutral
ports, and only gradually came to acquiesce in, what he could
not well prevent, the use by Nelson of an open roadstead on
the Sardinian coast.

Lastly, there was the eternal question of Algiers. That
pirate stronghold (for it could not be described otherwise)
lay as a continual menace to the Mediterranean communications. Neutral Italian vessels with valuable supplies were
always in danger of capture; the danger even to English

vessels was such as to call for convoy. With the declaration of war the Dey's insolence naturally increased inordinately: he knew he had no need to fear lest England should resort to war and bombardment, for she could not afford to have a dozen ships of the line crippled and out of action. Nelson's business was to keep the Dey in a good humour—it is significant, however, of what has been termed his recklessness, that the force he considered necessary to reduce the place was considerably greater than Exmouth found necessary in 1816.

Such, briefly, were the political problems with which Nelson had to deal on the spot; but no sooner had he joined his squadron off Toulon than problems of a more military and much more urgent nature clamoured for his attention. During the brief peace St Vincent had devoted himself to the task of retrenchment just as ferociously as ever he had assailed Frenchman or Spaniard. He had cut down expenditure below the level of efficiency. The nine ships of the line which Nelson found awaiting him were all in need of docking and repairs; their rigging was unserviceable, their stores were short, and every one was gravely short of men. The depots at Gibraltar and Malta were in as bad a case, and the continuous demands on them kept them for months after from accumulating any reserve at all. In Toulon there were several ships of the line ready for service, and there was always the chance of the arrival of others from the Atlantic. Nelson could not send his ships away in any number for refitting, even if there was any chance of getting it done. He was always troubled by the danger which threatens every blockading fleet—that it may be attacked at its 'average moment' by the enemy at his 'selected moment'.

He had to keep his forces massed and ready for instant action. For a period of nearly two years he did so, beginning, as we have seen, with every ship in bad order. During those two years the squadron as a body never saw the inside of a port. At the end of those two years the whole force at a moment's notice went off across the Atlantic and back again with a battle imminent at any moment. The achievement stands as nearly the greatest, and by far the least known, of all Nelson's claims to fame.

The fleet which Nelson commanded was, of course, only a fraction of the force which the Admiralty was using against the French. The task which was now being set to the British Government was the same as had presented itself to British Governments as far back as the days of Elizabeth and Henry VIII. At one end of the Channel lay a French army, large enough to do very serious harm in England, if not to conquer her altogether; at the other end, and in the Mediterranean, lay the ships of the line whose presence in the Straits of Dover was necessary if the army was to attempt the crossing. They were there because along the whole length of the Channel there was, on the French side, no suitable harbour for them—which was the main reason why Napoleon was expending millions on excavating a harbour out of the granite of Cherbourg. The most urgent duty of the British fleet, then, was to keep the French battle fleet away from the Straits of Dover, and the experience of centuries had proved that the best way of doing this was to station squadrons outside every port where French ships of the line were to be found, with a central reserve in the Channel itself both in case of accident and to keep the French flotillas harmless. To maintain these fleets at sea called for magnificent seamanship and much self-denial on the part of officers and men; it also meant considerable expense and a certain amount of loss. But if the expense could be borne and the loss made good, if the crews could endure the monotony and hardship of blockade, the reward lay not only in the continual

certainty of the whereabouts of the French fleet, but also in
the training of a magnificent school of seamen on the very
place where their battles were to be fought, a training which
the blockaded fleet could never provide for its officers and
men, who had, perforce, to learn the elements of their business in the unnatural and unreal surroundings of a sheltered
harbour. In 1803 the lesson had been taken well to heart.
The declaration of war sent the English squadrons flying
instantly to the places where experience had shown they
would be needed. Cornwallis took up position off Brest,
Collingwood off the Biscay coast; Keith commanded in the
Channel; Bickerton, on his own initiative, sailed for Toulon
with the Mediterranean squadron. It was the instant application of a well-tried method of solution to an old problem.

All the same, there were elements of risk and the certainty
of irritation. The sixty-six ships of the line which flew the
British ensign in 1803 were none too many for their task. All
the seven seas bore British shipping, and the ravages of
privateers and cruisers had to be guarded against and kept in
check. The Treaty of Amiens had given back to France and
her allies many of their outlying possessions, which now
afforded safe refuge to these pests. The French West Indian
islands were held by a large body of troops which not merely
made their reduction a matter of difficulty, but also constituted a standing menace to the British possessions.
Mauritius, the Cape, the Dutch East Indies were in a very
similar case. The British system of government resulted in a
peculiar sensitiveness to any blow delivered against her merchant shipping or her colonies. These were sources of wealth
which kept the ships of the line in action; but more, they
were the sources of wealth of the people who commanded
political influence. A Cabinet can hardly be blamed for considering its own existence as nearly as important as that of

the nation itself. Losses of merchant ships or colonies would mean grumbling in the City even if they did not endanger national life, and the Cabinet necessarily fought with one eye on the vitally important enemy—the fighting fleet—and the other on the commerce destroyers. The wonder was that they did so well. There are remarkably few instances of the dispersal of force for secondary objects; or, rather, the delicate balance between primary and secondary objects was usually accurately maintained.

To Napoleon, who now held the opposite ends of the threads of the puzzle, the puzzle which had been unsolved by Philip II and Louis XIV, by Madame de Pompadour and the Directory, the solution was not immediately obvious. His brilliant military instincts told him that the vital point was in the Straits of Dover, on whose coast he was gradually accumulating the finest army he ever commanded, but it was hard to see how to bring his strength to bear there. Wherever he turned there was always a little group of ships, tossed by the waves and scourged by the winds, as tiny in proportion to their surroundings as grains of dust on a parade ground, interposed between him and his desires. Yet it ought not to be difficult to lure these groups away from their stations. There were so many minor objectives open to him against which he could strike. Once get one of his squadrons loose, so that it vanished beyond the ken of the English intelligence into the ocean, and surely the British Admiralty, worried about the East Indies and the West, about Ireland and the merchant shipping, would seek to guard all these outlying limbs and so leave the heart exposed for a few crucial days. So he came confidently to expect, full of the contempt for any opponent who might set himself against him which scores of victories on land had developed. He began to weave the beginnings of those schemes which were to bulk so large in his

correspondence for the next two years. But Napoleon was a
tyro in the matter of naval warfare. He was pitting his inexperienced brains against those of men, not so great mentally
perhaps, who had spent their lives on the sea and who could
estimate chances far more accurately than he. All Napoleon's
plans in the end were landsman's plans, despite the tactful
and despairing pleadings of his naval advisers of real talent,
like Decrès, and Latouche-Tréville. Quite apart from practical flaws, such as his reliance upon the wind which brought a
relieving force to a port to bring out the ships within, his
plans invariably assume that his enemy will act rashly. At
Austerlitz he proved to be justified in his bold assumption
that his inexperienced enemies would commit themselves to
an eccentric movement and expose themselves to a crushing
counterblow, but never was this the case when he was pitted
against the canny clear-headedness of the British Admiralty
and the British Admirals. Never once did the evasion of a
French squadron bring about that hurried dispersal of British
strength to the four quarters of the earth which he confidently expected. And he was badly served by his instruments
too. They were just clever enough to realize the difficulties of
the task set them without being clever enough to propose a
satisfactory alternative or strong enough to refuse obedience.
And not one of them displayed the energy and moral courage
which would have been necessary to make good fighting
seamen out of the mixture of merchant seamen, landsmen
and soldiers which was all they were given for crews. To the
end of the war the British guns were fired at three times the
rate of the French ones, every broadside with considerably
more effect, while the tactical ideas of the British Captains
were a good deal clearer than those of the French—thanks
largely to Nelson—so that the British ships were brought into
action where their broadsides would be most effective.

A Nelson on the French side, a man with Nelson's energy and engaging personality, would have done much to alter this state of affairs. The guns would have been better served; the Captains, by prolonged discussion, would have become familiar enough with likely situations to anticipate the hostile attack by the vital five minutes. The French superiority of numbers would not have been so wasted.

By this time Nelson knew well what a blockade was like. He threw himself keenly into the business of keeping the fleet healthy and happy. The menace of scurvy had shown itself to be imminent in some of his ships, which had been in the Mediterranean for almost three years. That was not as serious now as it had been, because the remedy was better understood. From Sicily and Spain and Barbary Nelson wheedled invaluable stores of live beef and onions and oranges. Cruising over a wide area between the Balearic Isles, Sardinia and France, he gave his men as frequent a change of scene as possible, and variegated the monotony of the cruise as much as he could by encouraging dancing and theatrical performances. Repeatedly we find proud references to his success in this matter in his correspondence—'there are not six men in their beds in the fleet', 'we have not one sick in the whole fleet'. It was an astonishing achievement, one which would have startled Anson or Hawke, and one which compares very favourably even with modern experience; there were nearly ten thousand men under his command. The one bad sign which persisted for a considerable period was the frequency of desertion from ships in Spanish ports, and this must be attributed to the English disciplinary system, which made it possible for individual officers to harass men so that they were willing to leave the comparatively good food and good pay of the English service for the poor conditions and irregular pay of the Spanish.

The Government at home backed him up notably. The effect of St Vincent's ill-timed economies could not be expected to disappear for some time; the defects in ships and stores had to be borne with, but they gave him ample supplies of what he needed most—specie. For half a dozen years to come, until the Berlin decrees and the lavish subsidies in gold to the Continental powers had their effect, the central Government had plenty of gold to spare. And Nelson needed gold, to pay the agents who got him information and to buy those precious supplies of fresh food which were being secured in hole-and-corner fashion in neutral ports all round the western Mediterranean, wherein Treasury bills were not merely difficult of negotiation, but might bring decided trouble upon the heads of whatever governments or individuals might be found in possession of them. So that he was spared one constant source of annoyance which afflicted Wellington throughout the Peninsular War; although it is highly significant that Nelson, avid of responsibility as he usually was, only undertook with reluctance responsibility for money. In the matter of the blockade of Leghorn and Genoa he was well supported too, and his constant delicate negotiations with the Courts of Naples and Constantinople were approved both by the diplomatic representatives on the spot and by the Foreign Office at home.

The points of friction between Nelson and London were about the difficulty Nelson found in making satisfactory use of the force allowed him. He had too few frigates at his disposition. If he stationed east of Sicily the number he thought necessary, losses of merchant ships occurred in the west. When he brought back some, the French made captures from the Turkey fleet—and there was prompt complaint made to the Admiralty by the merchants who suffered. He wrote to the Admiralty for more frigates 'until I was tired'; he notes in a private letter that the Admiralty had left off answering those parts of his letters. The Admiralty simply had not the frigates to give him; every war has found England short of cruisers. It was only by the most persevering and ingenious economy in the employment of his small craft that Nelson was able to struggle along at all. He waited to send his despatches until he had a convoy to go with the ship that bore them. He sent off the ships which needed docking only at those times when they would cover merchant ships in their passage. The frigates which gathered information, at the same time scoured for privateers. Return journeys, planned of necessity months ahead, were ordered with the same object. He kept his scanty forces on the move ceaselessly, round and round the Mediterranean, and once or twice ill-advised orders from London, over his head, upset the whole precarious arrangement and annoyed Nelson exceedingly, although he realized that the Admiralty had not appreciated how delicate were the workings with which they were interfering.

He also was writing recommending that his excellent crews should be expanded by drafts of landsmen, and distributed over a larger number of newly refitted ships from home, but this again was impossible. St Vincent, hurriedly commissioning ships as fast as he could lay his hands on crews, officers and materials, simply could not spare them for any time for any elaborate re-arrangements. The ships, as fast as they could be commissioned in England, were hurried off on the spot to where there was pressing need for them. Nothing could be spared to Nelson for reinforcement or replacement, not even though occasionally his strength was down to four ships of the line while seven were ready in Toulon.

His private correspondence with Lady Hamilton at this period tells her of some of these troubles, but it is far more

taken up with hers. In the winter after his departure she
bore a still-born child of which it seems he was the father—
there appears to be no room for doubt about the birth,
although it is admittedly a good deal less documented than
that of Horatia Nelson Thompson—and she was already
hard pressed for money. Nelson was continuing to solicit a
pension for her (he could give her no more out of his own
pocket, for his own expenses were heavy), but, seeing that
her claim was based upon services which the Government
considered inconsiderable, he was unsuccessful. Nelson by
now had come to believe that she had been of much service
to England, but it seems likely that he was wrong; indeed, in
the matter of the claim that it was due to her management
that Nelson's fleet was supplied at Syracuse in 1798,
Nelson's own contemporary letters serve as disproof. When,
after Nelson's death, the codicil of his will in which he left
Emma as a 'legacy to his King and country', became public,
it was found that he still advanced these claims for a pension. Had he, instead, boldly declared himself the father of
her child, the result might have been different, but as it was
the Government could hardly be blamed for neglecting her,
especially as she was in possession of the annuity left her by
Hamilton, of Merton and of the large capital sums left her by
Nelson, and of various legacies left her by the Duke of
Queensberry and others. His letters to her are full of hope
and optimism; for the first few months not merely does he
not complain of the state of his health, but he declares hap-
pily that he has never been better in his life—which is only
what one would expect when one appreciates how busy he
was and how he delighted in hard work. He seems definitely
to have passed the madly besotted stage of his affection; his
letters are tender and kindly enough, but they lack the old
delirium of those written from the Baltic. Furthermore, it

seems that at last he had come to realize that his beloved
Emma might perhaps have faults—a possibility he would
have denied with furious indignation two years earlier. Yet,
all the same, such was his quixotic desire to do nothing to
rouse her jealousy that during all the weary cruise from Malta
onwards he never set foot on land.

Gradually, however, a change came over him; his health
began to droop and his optimism (his personal optimism only,
be it understood; his belief in the ultimate success of the
national cause never faltered) began to dwindle. The strain of
incessant desk work began to tell on him; he complains of
constant sea-sickness. The amount of work he was doing was
prodigious. It must be remembered that after Trafalgar had
been won the duties which fell upon Collingwood proved
eventually too much even for his iron frame, and he died at his
desk because of the refusal of the Admiralty to relieve him. So
that it will be the more readily appreciated how strenuous was
the Mediterranean command in these days, when the English
Navy was weaker and when at the same time it was
confronted by an enemy of growing strength and significant
activity. Thirteen months of toil saw the Mediterranean command in fair order; the men were healthy, the convoy system
was satisfactorily established, the anchorage off the Madalena
Islands (beside the Straits of Bonifacio) well known and its
use tolerated by the Sardinian Government, the political situation clearing up. After fifteen months in his new command
Nelson began to solicit an interval of leave; eventually permission came out to him to come home as soon as he wished.
Bickerton was to be given the command temporarily, and
Nelson was to resume it when he had recovered. Nelson did
not avail himself of the opportunity.

He himself says in his letters of this period that his health
had shown signs of improvement again; he may have changed

his mind solely on that account. It seems likely, however, that prospects of increased activity in the seas under his command had much to do both with his improvement in health and his altered decision. The Toulon fleet had begun to show itself out of its harbour. Latouche-Tréville had on one occasion brought his ships out to chase off a small English squadron which had followed a couple of his frigates close inshore; Nelson challenged action twenty miles to lee-ward with five ships of the line against eight (Bickerton was some distance off) and Latouche retired. Yet Latouche's account of the incident was that he had pursued throughout the night and saw no signs of his flying enemy next morning, and Nelson was fantastically annoyed when this report came to his ears. He swore he would make Latouche eat his words, literally, if ever he fell in with him, and he never forgave him, not even after Latouche's death. Both the desire to encounter Latouche and the indication this incident gave of a possible sortie by the French kept him to his post; more-over, as the summer of 1804 wore on it began to grow certain that Spain would enter the war. Her attitude began to dis-play the time-honoured vacillations. She extended liberal hospitality to French ships, and interpreted the neutrality laws more and more strictly against England, but she was clearly playing for time until the arrival of the treasure-ships from America, just as she always had done, and England, act-ing on old precedent, was determined to anticipate the inevitable declaration of war by a blow at the treasure fleet.

Soon after Nelson had been given permission to come home when it suited him, that section of his command extending from Gibraltar to Finisterre was taken from him and given to Sir John Orde (one of the two Admirals who had complained so bitterly against Nelson's command of the Mediterranean detachment which won the Battle of the

Nile), who was sent with half a dozen ships of the line and some frigates to await off Cadiz the arrival of the treasure-ships. It meant that Nelson was deprived of his chance of sharing in the prize money—his share might have amounted to anything up to a quarter of a million sterling—but actually, in view of his application for leave, he had no reason to complain. Complain he did at first, unreasonably, but he reconciled himself to the new conditions speedily enough, despite the fact that Orde announced to him his arrival on the new command with deplorably little tact.

In October, 1804, the treasure-ships were attacked. Three frigates out of four were taken, the other was sunk. At the news Nelson promptly issued orders for the detention of Spanish ships throughout his command, and began the business of establishing a fresh routine for his squadron to meet the altered conditions. The adjustments were speedily made—Nelson settled down once more to his continual cruising, to his continual sifting of intelligence, his continual making the most of inadequate means, his continual conferences with his Captains regarding the longed-for battle. News came that troops were being put on board the Toulon squadron; a move was certain soon.

CHAPTER XVI

THE PURSUIT

THEN at last, on January 19th, 1805, while Nelson's ships were rolling at their anchors in Madalena Roads in a heavy gale, his lookout frigates came racing into sight, flying the signal that the enemy was out. Villeneuve was beginning Napoleon's latest scheme for a concentration of force. By nightfall Nelson had weighed anchor and was sailing to intercept them; the French had last been seen that morning, west of Ajaccio, heading south-south-west under a press of sail before a north-westerly gale.

Once again arose the old problem of deducing their destination. It could be Sardinia or Sicily, Naples or Spain, Greece or Ireland, Egypt or the West Indies, or the Channel. No attempt was made on Sardinia, so that after three days of battling with the gale Nelson came down to Sicily, scattering his frigates, and even, perforce, his faster battleships far and wide for information. None came to him. With the wind as it still blew the French could only have gone east if they had not returned to Toulon. Eastward he went, then, as fast as he could drive his crazy ships through the wild sea, to Greece and Alexandria. He found nothing and beat his way back to Malta. There news awaited him at last. The French, sadly crippled by the unaccustomed gale, had put back to Toulon, much to Napoleon's fury.

Nelson struggled back to Sardinia again, through appalling weather. From thence he went, cunningly, to show himself off the coast of Spain, and then, dashing back to Sardinia, where in the Gulf of Palmas to the south-east of the island he began hurriedly to revictual his ships. No sooner had he done this and beaten his way out again to the westward than his frigates reported once more that the French were again at sea, having quitted port five days before. Villeneuve's orders were to avoid action, to unite with the Spanish squadrons at Cartagena and Cadiz, and to hurry to Martinique in the West Indies, where, if fortune were kind, he would before forty days be joined by the twenty ships of the Brest squadron. He headed eastward of the Balearic Isles, but, with much better luck than Nelson, he received news from a neutral of Nelson's presence at Palmas (his last report placed Nelson near Barcelona), so that, taking advantage of the easterly wind, he turned west, passed north of Minorca, and came down the east coast of Spain with favouring winds all the way. On March 30th he had left Toulon; by April 8th he was through the Straits.

Nelson, on the other hand, had no news at all. Had Villeneuve been as unlucky he would have fallen straight into Nelson's hands, for the latter continued to cruise to the westward of Sardinia until the 6th. On the 9th he was off Palermo, still with only negative information. He began to beat back against head winds for Toulon, until at last on the 18th, he received the news that Villeneuve had been seen off the coast of Spain to the southward of Malaga on the 8th. Furious with disappointment and anxiety, he turned westward in pursuit; he left his frigates to prevent the transport of small bodies of troops to Sardinia and Sicily, and he continued to struggle against head winds for day after weary day towards the Straits. Every day brought a head wind, although

until this time not a week had gone by without an easterly
one. Gibraltar was only reached by May 6th, but as soon as
he arrived there the wind shifted into the east, and the signal to get under way again was made before the whole fleet
had anchored. He pushed on to Cape St Vincent, and thence
to Lagos Bay, sending on ahead to Lisbon for news.

Villeneuve had not been able to induce any Spanish ships
to join him at Cartagena, but he had come down out of the
Mediterranean very unexpectedly for Admiral Orde off
Cadiz, driven away that officer and his small squadron, and
had united under his command the Spanish ships there.
Orde had six ships against eleven, or against eighteen if the
Cadiz squadron be included. He had acted in uninspired
fashion; having got his ships out of serious danger he went
straight northward to join the fleet blockading Brest—the
obvious thing to do, and a course which, if not brilliant, was
at least sound, as arranging for concentration at the vital
point. But he had made no attempt to ascertain Villeneuve's
further course; he had not clung to him for a day or two, as
any good officer might have done, and he had left no news
for Nelson following after. Apparently Orde did not think it
possible that Villeneuve would have any other design than a
movement northward, and Nelson came to complain bitterly
that Orde had lost what every Admiral desired so eagerly—
touch with an enemy who desired to avoid battle. As for
Orde, public clamour turned against him venomously, not for
losing touch, but for not fighting Villeneuve, which he was
quite right not to do. The agitation ended in Orde's resign-
ing the command which he had so earnestly solicited.

Nelson, at Lagos, found the same distressing absence of
information which had hampered him all the time. The fact
that Villeneuve had seven thousand troops on board made it
possible that he was headed for Ireland, where such a force

might set the country aflame from one sea to another, but there were no tidings of his having gone thither, and negative evidence is occasionally important. Hints gathered here and there—the most important came from an Englishman holding flag rank in the Portuguese Navy—led him to make a most momentous decision. He wrote, on May 10th, that he was taking his squadron off to the West Indies. If his guess proved to be wrong, it meant, seemingly for certain, his utter professional ruin. He remarks upon this possibility in his letters, but it did not deter him. If the French made a bad passage, he might overtake them; he would, at least, arrive in the West Indies before they had time to do much damage there. Should the two fleets meet, he could afford to wait, to manoeuvre, to bide his time until the unhandy enemy, with his ships manned by men of two nations, was caught at a disadvantage, as the Spaniards had been at St Vincent, and then he could fall upon them and do them damage enough to put them out of mischief even at the cost of serious loss to himself. His unexpected arrival would certainly upset the French plans. And, come what might, the Channel Fleet still held the interior position. He was risking little save his own reputation; he stood to gain much for his country. With these possibilities in his mind, but still without certain information, he urged his pursuit into the Atlantic, making use of every breath of wind; Keats of the *Superb*, the crankiest and slowest ship of all that battered squadron, lashed his studding-sail booms to his yards in a desperate effort not to delay the fleet too much, while Nelson, himself in a fever of haste and anxiety, sent him notes assuring him that he must not fret about the slowness of his ship. At last, on June 4th, they reached Barbados, and the uncertainty was at an end. Villeneuve had sailed for the West Indies; he had reached Martinique on May 14th. Nelson had gained ten days on him on the passage.

Villeneuve's fleet was very sickly; he put a thousand sick on shore on his arrival and he had buried hundreds more at sea before that. He did almost nothing during his brief stay. He picked up two more ships of the line; he captured a dozen sail of merchant shipping; he captured Diamond Rock (off Martinique) from the slender British garrison which had held it, much to the annoyance of the French for almost a year; then, when about to launch his first serious attack, upon Barbados, he heard of Nelson's arrival there. Villeneuve's imagination gave Nelson nineteen ships of the line—actually he had twelve by now—and Villeneuve was horrified by the news. He abandoned the West Indies. He abandoned all Napoleon's cherished plan of a huge concentration of strength there. Hurriedly despatching his troops hither and thither as garrisons for the islands (where they were eventually, of course, to fall as prisoners into English hands as soon as Trafalgar made it convenient for attack to be made on them), Villeneuve fled from the West Indies and from the dreaded name of Nelson; he yearned inexpressibly for the quiet minimum of comfort given by a blockaded port. In panic haste Villeneuve laid his course for France.

This time incorrect information, not lack of information, had prevented Nelson from forcing an encounter. His own plan had been to push straight on towards Martinique, where he could hardly have missed Villeneuve, but a hasty though exceedingly circumstantial message from General Brereton, at Santa Lucia, arrived to the effect that Villeneuve had been seen there going south a week before. Assuming at once that a blow against Trinidad was being planned, he dashed off to the southward, but at Trinidad he learned that no French fleet had been seen in the vicinity. 'Damn General Brereton', wrote Nelson to Davison. Coming back, he received accurate information at last of the French movements. From the scanty data—the landing of troops, the course taken by the French, and what was known of their previous movements— Nelson drew the instant and correct deduction that they were on their way to recross the Atlantic. The same night he came to the decision to follow. It was a brilliant piece of work. It is hard to decide which to admire most: the accuracy of the deduction, the self-confidence which believed in it, or the force of mind with which he brought himself to uncover England's most valuable colonial possessions solely on deductions made from a series of individually inconclusive facts. The loss of a sugar island or two might still wreck the career even of a Nelson.

Back came Nelson; even he could not guess whether the French were bound for the Straits of Gibraltar or the Biscay ports. But he knew that as long as a powerful British squadron held position outside Brest, junction between Villeneuve and the Biscay squadrons was impossible. He sent warning to Cornwallis, and he himself headed for Gibraltar, with every nerve at strain with waiting to hear that the French were in sight. They were not sighted in all that anxious return voyage, although at one time the French fleet was only a scant few score miles to the north-westward of Nelson at the Azores; but information from a neutral told him that his deduction was correct and that the French had been seen homeward bound. That neutral must have been either malicious or else more hazy than usual about his position, for the information seemed to indicate that Nelson was actually on the heels of the French— which made the disappointment all the more bitter when Cape Spartel was sighted and no French fleet. Nelson had hoped to engage Villeneuve's twenty ships with his own eleven (one was left in the West Indies) some distance out to sea. With plenty of time at his disposal and the finest seamen in the world under

his command, he hoped—and we cannot help thinking he
would not have been disappointed—to hang on to the
clumsy enemy, harassing him, worrying him, seizing some
opportunity of taking him at a disadvantage, and then crippling him so badly that he would be no danger in the future.
He could remember the actions under Hotham's command,
when such opportunities had arisen against the French, and
St Vincent, when the Spaniards had exposed themselves to a
stunning blow. He was justified in expecting a similar chance
to arise in the course of several days of contact with a fleet
of both French and Spaniards.

These chances and possibilities were discussed endlessly
in Nelson's cabin during the voyage. It is a pity that neither
Nelson nor his Captains were men of the pen. The fragments of memoranda which were written in this connection
and have survived are not very illuminating. They are significant; but, without the oral explanations with which Nelson
accompanied them and which roused his stolid Captains to
such enthusiasm, they are liable to varied interpretations,
none of them exceedingly original. That there was much
more about the plans made than we can read in the memoranda cannot be doubted; but Nelson had not the gift—an
exceedingly rare one—of describing a complicated situation
and involved manoeuvres in a few written words. He knew,
too, that the number of possibilities was so great that any
attempt to deal with each in detail would only defeat its own
object by burying the spirit of the orders in a mass of detail.
With his Captains accustomed to his methods of thought,
with the aid of his own example and a few signals, he knew
he could deal on the instant with any situation that arose.
Moreover, it seems that he appreciated his own ability to
think more clearly and rapidly in the midst of the heat and
danger of action—there are hints of this appreciation in his

letters—and he did not want to tie his own hands too much beforehand. But we are left to deplore the fact that none of his Captains had the desire or the ability to make notes which might survive of those many discussions and arguments immediately after taking part in them. The few fragments which we have we owe largely to Captain Keats of the *Superb*, who was not present at Trafalgar.

Villeneuve was safe from Nelson at the moment, and was hurrying, although with increasing infirmity of purpose, towards the Biscay ports. But the *Curieux*, the brig Nelson had sent with news of his movements from Antigua, fell in with him nine hundred miles from that place, made note of his course and his numbers, and raced on to England. She arrived at Plymouth on the 7th July, and her Captain rode with all speed he might to London. At the Admiralty he was brought into the presence of the new First Lord, Lord Barham, who had received a peerage in order to fill that position for a few months without seeking election to Parliament. Barham was an old man—he was seventy-nine at the time—but he was a man of supreme talent and decision, qualities he had already displayed during a long period (when he was Sir Charles Middleton) as Comptroller of the Navy. He realized in a flash the vital importance of Bettesworth's news; within a few hours he had dictated and despatched the orders which were to justify Nelson's pursuit and to ruin whatever there was practicable in Napoleon's orders. Within twelve days the English squadrons in the Bay of Biscay had taken advantage of their interior position, the blockades of Rochefort and Ferrol were momentarily suspended, and Calder with fifteen ships of the line, was off Cape Finisterre to intercept Villeneuve. Here, on July 22nd, the two fleets met. The weather was misty; there was no time to spare for elaborate manoeuvres. With allowance made for three-deckers, Calder's force was nearly equal to Villeneuve's; with allowance made for the poor order of the Spanish ships, it was certainly superior. But, instead of taking advantage of this great opportunity which Nelson had contrived for coming into contact with a fleet which had proved itself so elusive, Calder did not do everything possible for forcing a decisive battle. He was one of those officers at St Vincent who had considered Nelson's departure from the line as not quite the proper thing; the old prejudice seemed to affect him still. In a maze of mist, balked continually by variable winds, he tried to fight a battle in line, scorning the fierce mêlée which Nelson had so long envisaged. Two Spanish ships were cut off and captured, more to their captains' discredit than to Calder's credit, but the day was spent mainly in distant cannonading, which crippled English ships without bringing about close action. For three days afterwards the long-drawn-out game of hide and seek continued; some say that Calder displayed unnecessary anxiety about the safety of his two prizes. By the 26th of July Villeneuve had got clear, and on the 28th he dived into the grateful shelter of Vigo Bay, transferring most of his ships later, by the aid of good luck and with a poltroon's interpretation of Napoleon's orders, to Ferrol.

Calder, true at least to the guiding strategic principle of the English naval system, fell back, resumed the blockade of Rochefort, and joined Cornwallis off Brest with the greater part of his squadron. The very next day came Nelson with his magnificent eleven.

Nelson had reached Gibraltar two days before Calder's battle; there was no news yet of Villeneuve, which was an unpleasant shock. But, unwearied and undismayed, he set about revictualling and rewatering his ships—there had been no time for that during the nine days in the West Indies.

Scurvy, in fact, was beginning to make its appearance, but he crossed promptly to Tetuan to obtain fresh provisions. There he heard, by the arrival of a Lisbon newspaper, of the arrival of the *Curieux* in England, of the information she had brought, and of the dispositions brought about. An easterly wind was blowing to take them out of the Straits; the signal was made at once to weigh anchor, and the squadron dashed out once more—leaving all Nelson's washing, 'to my last shirt', on board the frigate which had brought the news. At Gibraltar he had set foot on land for the first time for almost two years, proof positive of his determination to remain true to his beloved Emma—also perhaps, it is not quite the same thing, of a desire to avoid, with a wisdom born of experience, all possibility of further entanglements.

Orders went out for the establishment of the blockade of Cartagena; information was despatched to Bickerton and Collingwood and Cornwallis even as the fleet weighed anchor. Heading northward again, they passed Collingwood maintaining his sleepless watch over Cadiz. Struggling on against adverse winds, they picked up scanty scraps of information here and there regarding Calder's action and Villeneuve's movements, and at last they reached Cornwallis. The years of blockade and the months of pursuit had brought Nelson no victory.

CHAPTER XVII

TRAFALGAR

NELSON had earned a rest after his two and a quarter years of strenuous service. What was more, he needed one. Cornwallis let him go without waste of time—he had held for nearly a year the Admiralty's permission to go on leave—and on August 18th he was at Portsmouth, hauling down his flag the next day.

The public gave him a great reception, the more striking as at the same time they were clamouring for Calder's recall and court-martial. Nelson had fought no battle, he had taken no ship of the line from the enemy, but the public had known him of old, knew him as a man who would fight, and who would seek to fight; his search for a battle across the Atlantic and back again, and his sudden appearance in the West Indies which had saved the situation there had caught the public's fancy. The Government received him with deference too. They had no fancy for Calders and Ordes; the uncanny way in which Nelson had divined his enemy's movements had impressed them deeply, and he was called upon repeatedly for his opinion and advice. When Villeneuve, goaded once more into movement by Napoleon's furious orders from Paris, escaped from Ferrol, Nelson had to give an opinion on the result of the battle which was expected between Villeneuve and Calder. He had to make suggestions about increasing the strictness of the blockade, and the suggestions made were two years later to blossom out into the Orders in Council of 1807. In the little while he was in England he certainly managed to do a large amount of work and to display inexhaustible interest in public, especially maritime, affairs.

His public life in this short month has been purposely considered before his private life. Various writers have represented him at this time as being anxious to leave the service for good and to settle quietly at Merton; reports, which may in the end be traced back to Lady Hamilton, state that it was her influence alone which led him to accept another command. They are quite without written evidence to back them. Nelson did, indeed, feel that his leave was too short, and that he needed further rest, but the tenor of his letters of this period, when they are all read carefully, does much to show that he was very willing—eager, in fact—to resume and complete his life's work of reducing the power of France. There are no letters of importance from Nelson to Emma at this time, of course, but there are plenty of other periods which go to prove that it was Lady Hamilton, not Nelson, who on most occasions was chary about his offering his services. And she had a powerful motive, too, in keeping him out of danger, for it was only the money he gave her which enabled her to live in anything like the fashion she desired. From all the evidence it seems as though he had grown beyond the really wantonly, mad phase of passion. There are several descriptions available of their attitude towards each other at this time, and they all go to prove that although he still loved her deeply, he had come to realize that he had no justification for putting her before his duty—he had been on the verge of thinking that in the dark days five years ago. The panegyrics which she lavished upon him to his face had lost a little of their savour—there is at least one circumstantial account of his cutting her short in public. There even seems to creep into the contemporary reports a vague series of hints—an atmosphere, not direct statement—that he was coming to love her much more when he was away from her than when he was with her.

And the fact remains that Nelson's further services were requested by the Admiralty, not especially volunteered by him, and at no time could Emma restrain Nelson from obeying such a request. England does not owe Trafalgar to Emma's self-sacrifice; which, after all, is nothing to the poor woman's discredit.

It seems certain, nevertheless, that Nelson was obsessed at the time of his departure with the presentiment of death. He told more persons than one that he would not be coming home again, and the deep melancholy which tinges his entries in his journal at this time seems to be due to more than sorrow at leaving Merton, Emma and Horatia. The presentiment was not new to him; it had proved unfounded at Santa Cruz and at the Nile, but the firmness of his conviction makes the sacrifice of his life at Trafalgar all the more touching.

Villeneuve had been located once more in Cadiz. He commanded there thirty-six sail of the line, and both the public and the Government felt uneasy with such a force concentrated ready for battle and no Nelson to oppose them. The blockade of Cadiz by sea, and the primitive nature of its communications by land, would soon take effect in making the position of the Franco-Spanish fleet most uncomfortable. The movement of British troops into the Mediterranean, where they would cause continual apprehension and where there was little naval force to hinder their free movement, would have its effect in inducing the central Government, if not the local command, to order another effort by the combined fleet. The appearance of strong British naval forces on the French and Italian coasts would be a further goad towards activity. Both rumour and evidence went to show that a sortie from Cadiz was probable and imminent. Every ship that could be spared must be sent to the fleet outside Cadiz. Nelson must go too. Everybody knew him now as the best fighting man whose flag was flying.

On the 13th of September, less than four weeks after his arrival at Portsmouth, he drove from his dear Merton, 'where I left all that I held dear in the world'. On the 14th he went on board the *Victory*, which had been refitting. On the 15th he was at sea again. On the 28th—the day before his birthday—he took over from Collingwood the command of twenty-six sail of the line. The fleet was as good as ever he wished for. The spirit of brotherhood among the officers which he had done so much to encourage was now such that he had made no use of the offer of the Admiralty of permission to select his own officers. Professionally there was none in the world to compare with them. The crews were in splendid health; he had no complaints whatever to make about their discipline and training. If the fleet was inferior in numbers to the enemy, the Admiralty had certainly reinforced it above the strength which Nelson had deemed possible, and more ships still were on the way. 'Only numbers can annihilate', wrote Nelson—at least, he wrote, characteristically, 'Numbers can only annihilate', but he meant the other—and he was most anxious to have a fleet large enough to destroy Villeneuve. The results of such destruction he could foresee clearly enough. It would give England such a naval superiority that no large French fleet would venture again from French ports; there would be English naval strength to spare for the successive reduction of hostile

colonies, of Martinique and Havana, of Mauritius and Java, so
that England's wealth would steadily increase and her
merchant ships traverse the seas without hindrance. Her navy
would expand steadily; the pressure of her remorseless blockade would increase week by week, her frigates would flaunt
the British ensign along every mile of French coast, while the
French ships rotted in harbour. The heavier the blow he could
strike now the sooner would this result be produced.

He was, of course, instantly plunged into the business of
inducing the blockaded fleet to come out. He had sent the
Euryalus on ahead to warn the fleet not to salute 'his arrival,
and later he ordered new-comers to pay him no salutes: he
wished the French to remain in ignorance of his growing
strength. He kept his main body out of sight of the town,
observing the enemy only with an inshore squadron—
although, as ever, he had not enough frigates for his needs.
He saw to it that the blockade of Cadiz was strictly carried
out, heartily endorsing Collingwood's harsh order for the
confiscation of neutral vessels trading to those ports close by,
whence their cargoes could be run into Cadiz in small coasters. He made plans for the employment of incendiary rock-
ets against the vessels in harbour; all this although he
guessed that Napoleon was making almost as great efforts as
Nelson himself to force Villeneuve's fleet out of Cadiz.

For the battle that would follow Nelson continued the system of careful planning which he had initiated in the pursuit
of Bonaparte in 1798 and which he had maintained during
the double passage of the Atlantic. The officers of the fleet
dined with him repeatedly. His vivid verbal explanation of
his wishes inflamed them to enthusiasm. He issued a memorandum in which he endeavoured to envisage the attack he
desired; it is notable, apart from the manoeuvres suggested,
for some pithy sentences which have become classic in naval

science. 'Thinking it almost impossible to bring a fleet of
forty sail of the line into line of battle in variable winds, thick
weather, and other circumstances which must occur . . . .
The order of sailing is to be the order of battle . . . .
Something must be left to chance; nothing is sure in a sea
fight above all others. . . . No captain can do very wrong if he
places his ship alongside that of an enemy.' The initial formation which he planned for the battle was of two wings and
an advanced squadron. He had it in mind to fall upon the
rear of the enemy with superior forces, crushing it before it
could be succoured by the van—staving off the latter, if need
be, by the action of one of his wings, most likely that commanded by himself. He gave his second in command, commanding the other wing, a free hand to crush the fragment
of the enemy's fleet cut off while this was happening.

It is a device which has more than once been employed by
the greater military minds. Napoleon himself made use of it
strategically in his boldest and most unlucky campaign, that
of Waterloo. Strategically, it has appeared with constant slight
variations in campaign after campaign—it bears with it the
essence of the idea of 'interior lines' beloved of the military
doctrinaire. Tactically there are fewer examples in land
warfare—although Austerlitz is a possible instance—and on
sea there are less still. There are hints of it, perhaps, in some
of the engagements in the Dutch wars, but with those slight
exceptions no other examples can be quoted. The will-o'-the-
wisp certainty that one man can direct the movements of a
large fleet in action has lured Admirals in every age into maintaining a single line—a single mass, at least—so that local
superiority is only to be gained by turning the enemy's flank
or by defiling past a single point of his line. And a quest after
these objectives, against an enemy reasonably well handled,
and certainly against an enemy unwilling to fight, can only

result in very considerable delay and postponement of action; while one of the surest lessons of naval history is that postponement of action means in nine cases out of ten no action at all. There is proof sufficient of Nelson's clearness of mind, of his originality of thought, and of his greatness of heart, in this memorandum; he realises, almost alone among his contemporaries, the evil of over-centralized command; he devises a plan to make use of a decentralized command; and, by decentralization, he is prepared to entrust some part of his reputation and achievement to a subordinate.

The whole idea which runs through the memorandum is of gaining a local superiority which the enemy would not be able to neutralize quickly, in consequence of weather conditions and Nelson's own action. The gaining of local superiority is the first, the most easily stated, object of a commander; but it must be remembered that in those days Admirals had given up striving after it, thinking it to be too dangerous or difficult to obtain—especially when they had not implicit trust in their subordinates' readiness to carry out their designs, whether from unwillingness or inability to understand their superior's imperfectly voiced designs. Clerk of Eldin had tried to indicate methods of gaining local superiority, and Nelson had studied his suggestions. The Battle of the Saints had been a chancy, unexploited effort to fight on these lines; the Nile had been a very special case against a fleet at anchor. Never yet since the Dutch wars had there been a deliberate breaking up of a fleet into separate divisions with the express object of closing only with a part of the enemy. It was a revolutionary idea; so novel that Keats, an intelligent and active-minded officer, asked for time to think it over before he offered an opinion on it. The novelty of the plan is frequently lost sight of nowadays, when the formation of the fleet at Trafalgar is familiar to every mind. It should always be remembered that Trafalgar was the first example of such a battle—Nelson, as usual, was risking his reputation for his convictions. Long after Trafalgar the Admiralty went so far as to endorse his idea by inserting in the signal book a special signal ordering a similar manoeuvre, but it was never employed in action by a British fleet. The French, as a matter of fact, made use of a very similar attack at the bloody little Battle of Lissa, but they met with no success, being beaten off with severe loss by the English line.

Comparison is hard, but it seems nevertheless a source of disappointment that a hundred years later the battle orders, when Jutland was fought, although nominally giving the fullest possible independence to officers commanding divisions, still actually enforced a formation in line, seven miles of ships, rigid and difficult to handle, which failed (there is no gainsaying it) in its primary object of compelling the enemy to fight. The Germans got away without much hurt. The question of burning importance is whether a Nelson in command of the British fleet would have been able to force a battle advantageously, and every one is allowed his own individual opinion as to what the answer should be.

Rumour grew apace that the French and Spaniards were coming out. Despite this, Nelson was compelled to send a detachment to Gibraltar to complete with stores. He had to have his fleet ready for instant service of any possible nature; he could not possibly allow it to run short of supplies. It was the problem which vexed Admirals commanding blockading fleets for centuries before and was to do so for generations later—the blockading fleet is always weakened by these necessary detachments, while the blockaded fleet can choose its own moment and sally in full force. This reduction in Nelson's strength was necessary; he made another which was by no means equally necessary. Calder had to go home for

court-martial; dissatisfaction with his conduct had increased
with each new discovery regarding the enemy's movements.
To Nelson had been given the task of informing Calder of his
recall—until then the latter had apparently been quite satisfied with his achievements, although he had asked for an
inquiry—and of the Admiralty's order that he should shift his
flag to a smaller vessel for the voyage home. The poor man
was quite stunned by the news. He was horrified at hearing
that he would have to go home in a frigate with these charges
awaiting him. He begged Nelson to allow him permission to
make the voyage in his three-decker flagship (it is easy to
remember a time when Nelson bundled himself and his staff
into a frigate at a moment's notice), and Nelson yielded at
last, reluctantly and not without misgivings and after chang-
ing his mind at least once. He displayed the utmost kindness
and consideration for the unhappy man, despite the poor
opinion he held both of his talents and of his achievements.
It was a melancholy business, for there was more than a
chance that Calder might meet the fate of Byng, although as
things happened Calder escaped with censure.

Fortunately the arrival of four more ships from England
brought the numbers up to a respectable figure once
more, twenty-seven of the line, seven of them of three
decks. Against these Villeneuve could bring thirty-three,
including four three-deckers. Counting a three-decker as
worth two two-deckers (which was done fairly generally at
this period), Nelson commanded thirty-four units against
thirty-seven—not a very inferior force; but fifteen of
Villeneuve's fleet, including all the three-deckers, were
Spanish, and by Napoleon's own reckoning one French ship
was worth two Spanish ones, so that Villeneuve's fleet can
only be counted as twenty-eight units, and as greatly inferior
to Nelson's. The difficulties due to difference of nationality

in the allied fleet had been fairly overcome. Villeneuve held as much authority over Gravina as Paris held over Madrid, which is saying much. The ships of the two nationalities had been mingled together indiscriminately; curiously enough Villeneuve, like Nelson, had thought of employing a detached squadron of fast ships to hinder Nelson's manoeuvres; and it was, in the hour of battle, to meet the same experience as Nelson's and to be drawn at once into the fighting line.

For three weeks Nelson had beaten to and from the Atlantic engaged upon his multifarious duties, holding away as much as fifty miles from Cadiz for fear lest a westerly wind should force his unwieldy three-deckers through the Straits.

Then at last, at dawn on October 19th, Blackwood, in command of the inshore frigates, saw that the enemy was beginning to work his way out of port. By half-past nine the signal had been passed along the chain of transmitting ships and was received in the *Victory*, and the order was issued for the ships to chase south-eastwards to make sure that Villeneuve would not escape into the Mediterranean unfought. Nelson wrote his last letters to Lady Hamilton and Horatia (signing himself, 'your Father' to the latter) and awaited, with the utmost confidence, the approaching collision between the fleets, even while he was praying, with all the fervour of his strong belief, for God's help. All that day the fleet beat slowly south-eastwards against the faint southerly airs, while all that day the French and Spaniards were warping and towing their ships out of Cadiz harbour. When the next dawn came the British fleet was well up towards the Straits' mouth, shrouded in mist, and the last French ships were emerging from the harbour. Nelson had hardly left the *Victory*'s quarter-deck, although now he added a postscript to his letter to his 'dearest beloved Emma, dear friend of my bosom'. The wind worked round south-westerly, but still the fleets did not come into contact. Signals passed backwards and forwards between the frigates and the main body; Blackwood did his work admirably and kept Nelson fully informed of each successive movement of the enemy, while Nelson devised a code of night signals with him to convey instantly information of Villeneuve's course during the night.

No attempt had been made to fall on one part of the Franco-Spanish fleet while the remainder was still inside Cadiz. The underlying idea of all Nelson's plans had been to induce as many ships of the enemy to leave port as possible, and then to fall upon them when battle could not be refused. The course he set on October 19th and 20th was planned to this end; and when, soon after midday on the 20th, the wind backed still further round to west-north-west, with every sign of remaining there until the gale which threatened had blown itself out, Nelson knew his design was accomplished.

Villeneuve had only emerged from Cadiz reluctantly. He had little faith in himself and none in his allies. He knew that his half-hearted attempt to obey Napoleon's orders and effect a great combination at Brest had failed disastrously; he knew too, perhaps, that whatever other move he had effected in obedience to Napoleon would only have ended in worse disaster. To come out and court battle in the way he was doing—for he had no hope of gaining the Mediterranean without fighting—was to invite total defeat; he had few illusions on the point. Yet if he remained in port he could do nothing to avert the disaster, and he might well bring down upon himself the uttermost lightnings of Napoleon's wrath. Admiral Rosily was on his way to Cadiz by road; but for an accident to his carriage at Madrid, on October 14th, he would already have arrived, and Villeneuve would have been on his way to France, to trial, to lifelong imprisonment or death—or to the suicide's end which he sought two years later when actually he reached France. Rosily would take the fleet out to battle. Villeneuve would at least anticipate him; a miracle might give him victory. Great good luck might enable him to escape after a scrambling fight which would show Napoleon how hopeless were his orders for a pitched battle, and which at the same time would not utterly ruin the allied fleet. It was in this despairing, not even desperate state of mind that Villeneuve brought out his ships. The frigates that hung on to him by day and night left him without hope of escape through the Straits; he kept his straggling fleet massed as far as possible close up to his flagship, and struggled on through the midst. At dawn on the 21st the two fleets were just in sight of each other and of Cape Trafalgar, and the British fleet lay to windward.

Nelson was already on deck; he wore, as he constantly did, his uniform coat with its Orders—the Bath, the Crescent, and the two Neapolitan Orders. He commanded signals for order of sailing and preparation for battle. Then, in his cabin, amid the din the crew made while knocking down bulkheads and clearing for action, he wrote his last prayer in his journal and his last codicil to his will, drawing attention to Emma Hamilton's services to England, and leaving her to the beneficence of her country. He did not pray only by writing in his journal; a junior officer coming hastily through the curtain which had been hung in place of the bulkhead found him on his knees imploring his Maker's forgiveness and help.

The frigate Captains came on board with their reports; Hardy and Blackwood witnessed his signature to the codicil of the will; the two fleets were gradually nearing each other as the English ships set all possible sail before the faint breeze. Villeneuve had tried to form his five columns into a

single line at sight of the English; his inexperienced Captains
had not been very successful in making use of the slight wind,
and only a muddled crescent was ever formed. He signalled
to his ships to wear together, so as to stretch back again
towards Cadiz; so inefficiently was the order carried out that
Nelson believed them to be wearing in succession.

The wind was faint; the weather was thick. To Nelson's
mind it became apparent that if action were much longer
postponed the enemy might still think better of it and
return to Cadiz; certainly at every moment they were getting
nearer that place. His fleet was in two lines; in the van of
each were powerful three-deckers, almost unsinkable, built
to take and give the utmost punishment. He could see with
his own eye the wretchedly poor manoeuvring power of the
enemy. With brilliant ingenuity he substituted, for the original plan of holding off the French van while Collingwood
assailed the rear, the design of breaking into the hostile line
with the heads of his two columns. It would mean sad loss
for the leaders, but they were big ships and could bear it. On
the other hand, it would mean that two-thirds of the Franco-
Spanish fleet would be cut off and forced into a mêlée; he
reckoned—and advisedly as it proved—on the ill will and
unhandiness of the French van to postpone their entry into
action until the decisive moment was past. Every sail possible, even studding sails, was set so that the columns should
only endure for the shortest possible time the raking fire of
the enemy. Ordinarily when going into action a ship reduced
sail to 'fighting sails'; in the *Victory*, as she neared the French
line, Nelson berated an officer for taking in a lee lower studding sail in order to reset it properly.

The light winds and thick weather which Nelson had
anticipated in his memoranda were prevailing at the
moment. To form his 'advanced squadron' and his wings

would take time—an interminable time, if past experience was reliable. Brilliant reading of his opponent's mind told Nelson that delay might result in Villeneuve's will failing him and in a retreat—inglorious, but highly irritating to the English—back to Cadiz. Moreover, the obvious clumsiness and unhandiness of the enemy seemed to show that elaboration of manoeuvre would be unnecessary. The more rapid the blow, the more unready would be the enemy. A fierce attack, launched in this fashion in an unusual formation, would bear with it more of the elements of surprise than might be expected of an attack made when two fleets had practically been in presence for three days together.

On the other hand, there was present the danger that always must attend the execution of a novel plan in presence of the enemy. If his officers did not grasp his designs, and if they did not execute them with skill, there was a chance that the English fleet might come down in a muddled, disorderly fashion and be exposed to serious loss or a damaging repulse. Nelson bore the whole responsibility and must receive the whole credit that this did not occur—there are plenty of examples in English naval history of muddled attacks defeated in detail. But Nelson knew the officers under his command. He knew the extent of their professional skill, he knew their unreserved loyalty to himself and to each other, and he knew that they were so imbued with his ideas that they would instantly appreciate his intentions. For this knowledge he must receive credit; for the fact that his Captains so understood him he must receive more still. The old arrogant days of Byng—or even of Jervis, for that matter—were over. Nelson's genius had changed the ponderous but unwieldy bludgeon which once typified an English fleet into a flexible and far more deadly rapier, whose blade carried out instantly every thought of the mind that wielded it.

Largely it was a result only of a moral change, an atmospheric change, but few and fortunate are the personalities who can so temper the rigidity of the tradition of a fighting service. That discipline did not suffer through Nelson's new attitude Trafalgar is sufficient proof.

Yet all the same, even when full justice is done to Nelson's personal brilliance and achievement, there is room for admiration of the iron men who took their ships down into action in so unhesitating a fashion. There was room for failure even now, for the kind of clumsy rashness which has so often typified the Englishman in war that the unthinking have deemed it a virtue—the rashness of Minden, of Fontenoy, or of the Somme. But the English Captains fought the battle just as Nelson would have had it fought, and there can be no higher praise than that. Collingwood, as we shall see, even grumbled at the number of signals which Nelson considered necessary—few enough, in all conscience—and took his line down into action at exactly the point Nelson desired, calling forth Nelson's ready and outspoken praise on the instant. He took advantage of the crescent-shaped formation of the allied line—something the memoranda had not foreseen—to close more immediately and decisively with the rear by a more diagonal attack, 'lasking', so that his blow was more widely embracing at the moment of contact and a stronger grip obtained on the hesitant allied fleet.

Nelson had realized, with the rapidity of thought which was so peculiarly his, the extent of the opportunity presented to him, and the nature of the circumstances of the special case at the moment. He had the brain to plan and the moral courage to act; he could reap the reward not only of his former brilliance in command, but also of the less conspicuous achievements on which stress has been laid two paragraphs back. He gathered his fleet into his hand and sent it, in two long columns, headlong upon the ramshackle allied line.

Then came the signal 'England expects', altered for a variety of reasons from 'Nelson confides'. Collingwood began, as the first signal hoist was seen, to exclaim against Nelson's continuous signalling—although for the most important naval battle of the war the signals were curiously few—but he checked himself when he saw the purport of the message, and applied himself once more with his bold initiative to his duty of getting his line into action. The *Royal Sovereign*, new coppered and the best sailer in the fleet, approached the enemy's line soon after noon, and with this beginning of the battle the enemy hoisted his flags, and Nelson, at last able to distinguish Villeneuve's flagship, was able to direct the *Victory*'s course towards her. Nelson could see Collingwood bursting into the enemy's line; he could see the enemy's van still straggling ahead, Captains and Admirals alike without the intuition to guess the point at which he was striking nor with the quickness of mind to wear round early enough to save the situation. The attack was obviously promising. Collingwood had carried out his part with magnificent initiative; every Captain clearly knew his duty and would perform it as Nelson wished him to do.

Already the enemy's line had opened fire upon the *Victory*. The *Téméraire* had already tried for the place of honour at the head of the line and had not been successful. At least six ships had opened a deliberate and concentrated fire upon the advancing *Victory*. Her sails and rigging were being gradually shot to pieces. Blackwood reluctantly quitted the ship to return to his frigate. 'God bless you, Blackwood, I shall never speak to you again', said Nelson, with the presentiment of death growing steadily stronger. Casualties were occurring on deck; the wheel was shot away, the mizzen topmast fell, Hardy at Nelson's side was struck on the foot by a splinter. Still the *Victory* crawled slowly on. She reached the enemy's line. She beat the unfortunate *Bucentaure* into an utter wreck with her first deadly raking broadside. Balked in her attempt to fall alongside her by the self-sacrifice of the *Redoutable*, she fell on board the latter, with every gun in action and the clouds of smoke eddying round her. The smoke gathered thicker and thicker round the grappled fleets as the English ships came pressing up in succession into action.

The pride with which all three combatant nations remember that day is justified by the splendid courage displayed even in the beaten fleet. Frenchmen and Spaniards fought their guns to the end despite losses which rose in some ships to an almost unbelievable percentage. But the guns they worked were not as effective as were the English guns. Questions of material apart, French and Spaniards were not such good gunners. They could not serve their guns as quickly as the English; their aim (and aim counted for something in the opening stages of the battle when the English columns were coming down) was not as good; in the ebb and flow of the battle, when the flaws of wind swayed the partly dismasted hulls backwards and forwards, the officers' seamanship was not good enough to wring the utmost advantage from chance dispositions. And the balance of numbers, at least in this, the vital part of the battle, was against them. Nelson's bold inspiration had solved that eternal problem of how to bring a fleet into contact with an inferior part of an enemy's fleet (at a cost, gladly paid, beyond doubt, of frightful casualties in the leading ships), and the centre and rear of the allied line were cut off and exposed to the attack of the whole English fleet. Something—but not much—now depended on the behaviour of the van. A capable flag-officer there, who, with an inspiration equal to Nelson's, could guess the point of attack, and with ships instantly handy and perfectly handled could have reached that point with the utmost expedition, might have done much towards retrieving the initial disadvantage brought about by Nelson's skill and Villeneuve's apathy; nobody dare imagine he would have converted defeat into victory. But Nelson had foreseen the inexperienced slowness of wit of the French captains and flag-officers.

The French van mistook its duty. The French centre and rear, outnumbered and overwhelmed, was within five hours beaten into ruin and surrender.

But before that five hours had elapsed Nelson had been struck by a musket bullet from the *Redoutable*. Shoulder and spine shattered, he had been carried below, into the infernal heat of the cockpit, where the dim lanterns swayed and shook in the blinding smoke to every discharge of the *Victory*'s guns. Then followed the three hours of excruciating agony, when 'a victory being reported to Vice-Admiral Lord Viscount Nelson he then died of his wounds'.

INDEX

Family relationships are to Nelson

Abbreviations
Cdre = Commodore; Fr = France; HMS
= His Majesty's Ship; Rev = Reverend;
Sp = Spain; USA = United States of
America; V/A = Vice-Admiral

Aboukir Bay 115-16
  see also Nile, battle of the
Acre 135
Active, HMS 95
Acton, Sir John 60, 134
Agamemnon, HMS 30, 50, 58, 60-2, 65, 68,
  70-83, 162-3
Albemarle, HMS 27-9
Alcide (Fr) 78
Alexander, HMS 107-8, 111, 118
Alexandria 112-13, 122, 134-7, 144, 198
  blockade of 137, 144
Algiers 185-6
Amiens, Peace of 176, 179, 181, 188
Amphion, HMS 183
Andrews, Miss 34, 45-6, 104
Antigua 41-3, 205
Apulia 184
Arctic 13-14
Austerlitz, battle of 190, 213
Austria 8, 71, 77-80, 82, 85, 105, 124,
  129-30, 132, 146, 151, 157, 171, 185
Azores 203

Badger, HMS 22
Ball, Captain Edward 108, 123, 128,
  133-4, 178

Baltic Sea 28, 157-70, 175, 194
Barbados 201-2
Barbary Coast 185-6, 191
Barcelona 87
Barham, Admiral Lord 205
Bastia 65-7, 85, 88, 123
Bath 27, 46, 49, 103, 105
Beckford, William 154
Bellona, HMS 162-3
Berry, Captain Sir Edward 91, 104, 108,
  119, 138
Berwick, HMS 77
Bickerton, V/A Sir Richard 28, 183, 188,
  195-6, 207
Black Sea 111
Blackwood, Captain Sir Henry 217-19,
  223
Blanche, HMS 86
Blenheim, HMS 90
blockades 15, 51-3, 158, 160, 186, 188,
  191, 215
  see also under Corsica, Egypt, France,
    Malta, Syria, USA *and individual ports*
Boreas, HMS 35-44, 46
Bottesworth, Captain 205
Boulogne 173, 175
Brereton, General 202
Brest 76, 106-7, 137, 183, 199, 218
  blockade of 27, 143, 188, 200, 203, 209
Brindisi 184
Bristol, HMS 22
Bronté 4, 124, 144-5, 172, 176-8, 180
Brueys, Admiral 116-18
Bruix, Admiral 138, 145
Bucentaure (Fr) 224

Burgoyne, General 15-16
Byng, Admiral John 10, 18, 20, 116, 216, 221

Ça Ira (Fr) 74-5
Cadiz 53-4, 88, 92, 94-6, 102, 106-7, 183, 197, 199-200, 210-11, 217-18, 220-1
blockade of 94-6, 207, 210, 212
Cagliari 61
Calabria 136
Calder, Admiral Sir Robert 53, 205-8, 215-16
Calvi 64, 67
siege of 68-70, 88
Camperdown, battle of 106, 115, 179
Cape Finisterre 205-6
Cape St Vincent 200
battle of 3, 89-93, 95, 104-5, 109, 120, 158, 179, 201, 204, 206
Capraja 84
Captain, HMS 83, 88-91, 95, 104-5
Capua 142-4
Caracciolo, Francesco 141
Carcass, HMS 13-14
Cartagena 86-7, 107, 142, 199-200, 207
Censeur (Fr) 75
Charles Emmanuel IV, King of Sardinia 60, 185
Cherbourg 187
Chesapeake Bay, battle of 31
Choiseul, Duc de 16
Clerk of Eldin, John 19, 214
Codrington, Admiral 14
Cole, V/A 170
Collingwood, Cuthbert, Admiral 4, 37-8, 82, 91, 188, 195, 207, 211, 213, 220, 222-3
Conquérant (Fr) 118
Constantinople 114, 122, 147, 192
convoys 3, 28, 54, 61-2, 71-2, 144, 193, 195
Copenhagen
first battle of 2, 160-7, 172, 179
second battle of 166
Cordova, Admiral 92
Corfu 183-4
Cornwallis, Admiral Sir William 4, 19-20, 27, 183, 188, 203, 206-8
Cornwallis, General Charles, Lord 31
Corsica 62, 64-70, 72, 76, 78, 82, 84-5, 111, 185, 198

blockade of 62, 64, 67
British evacuation of 87, 92
see also Bastia, Calvi, San Fiorenzo
Corunna 52-3, 67
Crete 113-14
Cuba 32, 212
Culloden, HMS 89-90, 98, 105, 117-18, 123
Curieux, HMS 205, 207

Daedalus, HMS 29
Dalling, Governor 24-6
d'Aubant, General 67
Davison, Mr 168, 202
de Burgh, General 98
de Vins, General 78, 80
Decrès, Admiral 190
Defence, HMS 118
Denmark 157-67
d'Estaing, Admiral 24
Digby, Admiral 29-30
Dresden 152, 154
Duckworth, Admiral Sir John 137-8
Duncan, Admiral Sir John 106
Dundas, General Thomas 65-7
Dunkirk 173

East Indies 14, 28, 35, 188-9, 212
Egypt 183
blockade of 123, 136
French in 56, 73, 116-23, 134-5
see also Alexandria, Nile *and under* Napoleon
Elba 84, 86, 95, 97
Elephant, HMS 161-4
Elgin, Lord 147
Elliott, Sir Gilbert 65, 69, 84, 87, 94
Euryalus, HMS 212
Excellent, HMS 91-2

Favourite, HMS 95
Ferdinand I, King of Naples 5, 60, 129-31, 137, 139-42, 144, 151
Ferrol 53, 205-6, 208
Fischer, Cdre 169
Fitzharris, Lord 152
Foley, Captain 117-18, 161, 163
Foote, Captain 139, 141
Foudroyant, HMS 104, 138, 140-2, 144, 146-8, 151
Fox, HMS 100

France
  American War of Independence 21
  blockade of 51-3, 55, 171, 188, 205
  French Revolution 32, 50, 55-6, 65
  naval tactics and strategy 18-20, 55, 72, 75
  state of Navy 16-18, 55-6, 116, 120, 181, 190, 220
Francis, Crown Prince of Naples 139
Freemantle, Captain 96
Freemantle, Mrs 100
Fremantle, Captain 84

Gaeta 142, 144
Garrat, Citoyen 127
Généreux (Fr) 146
Genoa 59, 72, 77, 79, 82-6, 146, 181, 183, 185
  blockade of 62, 79-81, 192
George III, King of England 5, 15, 32, 65, 77, 103-4, 140, 154, 169
George, Prince of Wales 5, 48, 169-70, 172
Geraldino, Cdre 91
Germain, General Lord George 15
Gibraltar 31, 86-7, 95, 107-9, 123, 183, 186, 199-200, 203, 206-7, 215, 217
Glorious First of June, battle of 71, 77, 106
Godoy, Manuel de 84, 106
Goliath, HMS 117-18
Goodall, Admiral Samuel 76
Grasse, Admiral 31
Graves, Admiral Sir Thomas 167
Graves, Admiral Thomas 31
Gravina, Admiral 217
Greece 111, 184-5, 198
Greville, Charles 125-6, 145, 149, 169-70, 173, 177, 180
Guerrier (Fr) 118
Guillaume Tell (Fr) 146-7
gunnery 18-20, 55, 75, 90, 163, 164-5, 190, 224

Hallowell, Captain 123
Hamilton, Emma Lady 3-6, 8, 10, 47, 60, 114, 124-8, 130, 132-3, 135-6, 139, 141-5, 147-55, 159, 169, 172-80, 193-5, 209, 217, 219
Hamilton, Sir William 6, 60, 112, 125-7, 133, 135-6, 139-43, 145-55, 169-70,
    172-3, 176-9, 181, 194
  death of 180, 182
Hardy, Captain Thomas 87-8, 108, 219, 223-4
Herbert, Mr 45-6
Hinchinbrook, HMS 23-4
Hohenlinden, battle of 157
Hood, Admiral Lord 21, 29-30, 32, 48-9, 58-60, 62, 64-70, 73, 76, 103, 121, 158, 178, 181
Hood, V/A Sir Samuel 123, 134
Hotham, Admiral William 68, 73, 75-9, 81, 204
Howe, Admiral Lord 15-16, 33, 35, 71
Hughes, Admiral Sir Richard 28, 35, 37-43, 45
Hunt, Captain 69

India 122
Ireland 107, 111, 189, 200-1
Irresistible, HMS 95

Jamaica 14, 22, 23-4, 24, 27, 43, 158
Janus, HMS 26-7
Jervis, Admiral Sir John, Earl of St Vincent 6, 81, 83-7, 89-95, 97-8, 102-4, 106-7, 109-11, 114-15, 119, 121-2, 124, 135, 138-9, 158, 167, 173-5, 181, 186, 192-3, 221

Keats, Captain 201, 205, 214
Keith, Admiral Lord 10, 47, 138-9, 142-3, 145-7, 151, 154
Keppel, Admiral Lord 20
Kronstadt 160, 168

La Galissonière, Admiral 18
Langara, Admiral Juan de 59
Latouche-Tréville, Admiral 190, 196
League of Armed Neutrality 157-8, 166
Leander, HMS 138
Leeward Islands 35, 37-8, 49
Leghorn 61-2, 64, 70, 73, 81-2, 84, 130, 132, 146, 151, 183, 192
Linzee, Cdre 61-2
Lion, HMS 27
Lissa, battle of 215
Livorno see Leghorn
Locker, Captain 22, 27, 48
Lodi, battle of 83
Lombardy 144, 181

Louis, Captain 119, 144
Lowestoft, HMS 14, 22, 27
Lutwidge, Captain 13

Mack, General 129-31
Madalena Islands 195, 198
Malta 112, 128-9, 133-4, 137, 144, 148,
    181-3, 186, 195
    blockade of 128, 134-5, 138, 144,
    146-7, 151
Man, Admiral 76, 78, 86
Mantua 83
Marengo, battle of 56, 152, 157
Maria Carolina, Queen of Naples 5,
    126-7, 129-31, 137, 151-2
Maritimo 137
Marlborough, Duke of 179
Martinique 199, 201-2, 212
Masséna, Marshal 146
Mathews, Admiral 20, 90
Mauritius 188, 212
Merton 176-8, 181-3, 194, 209-11
Milan 83, 105
Milford Haven 125, 173, 177, 179
Miller, Captain 91
Millesimo, battle of 82
Minerve, HMS 86-8
Minorca 10, 18, 20, 31, 64-5, 76, 87,
    137-9, 142, 199
Minotaur, HMS 118
Minto, Lord 178
Montenotte, battle of 82
Moore, Sir John 67
Morea 111, 114
Moutray, Captain 41-2
Moutray, Mrs 42, 46, 128
Mutine, HMS 108, 112, 127
mutinies 8, 93, 97

Naples 60, 66, 73, 76, 80, 84-5, 87-8,
    111-12, 114, 124-32, 133, 136-7,
    138-9, 142, 144, 148-9, 180, 183-4,
    192, 194, 198
    rebellion in 136-42
Napoleon I, Emperor of the French 1-2,
    7-8, 12, 56, 61, 63, 73, 80, 82-3, 105,
    110, 112, 116, 179, 184, 205-6, 208,
    212-13, 216, 218-19
    and expedition to Egypt 113, 116-21,
    127, 212
    and invasion of England 171-5, 187,

189-90, 198, 202, 211
Naval Chronicle 6
Navigation Acts 37-41, 45, 48
Nelson, Rev Edmund (father) 12, 103,
    145, 153, 167, 178-9
Nelson, Frances Lady (wife) 6, 46-8, 67,
    70, 94, 103, 105, 107, 119, 128, 148,
    153, 155-6, 168-9, 182
Nelson, Horatia (daughter) 154-6, 159,
    194, 210, 217
Nelson, V/A Horatio
    appearance 155, 178
    attitude to France 5-6
    character 1-11, 13-14, 29-30, 34, 41-3,
        46-7, 69, 74, 78, 94, 96, 104, 109,
        113, 121, 128, 135-6, 143, 145-6,
        149, 161, 164, 195, 203, 210, 219,
        222
    childhood 3-4, 7-9
    children 154-6, 194
    courtships and marriage 34-5, 37, 45-8,
        168-9
    death of 225
    discipline 8, 36, 58-9
    finances 103-4, 120-1, 123, 136, 144-5,
        177-9, 181-2, 194, 209
    health 14, 26-8, 104, 122-3, 128, 146-7,
        155, 175-6, 194-5, 195-6
    honours 9, 120, 124, 131, 144-5, 148,
        167, 178, 219
    and Lady Hamilton 124, 127-8, 132,
        141, 144, 148-9, 151-6, 159, 168-70,
        172-6, 181-2, 193-5, 207, 209-10,
        217-19
    letters 1-11, 27, 42, 44, 46-7, 67, 69,
        74, 81, 96, 103, 107, 112, 119, 122-3,
        146-8, 155, 159, 193-6, 201, 204-5,
        209, 211, 217
    naval training 12-15, 17, 20-1
    promoted Captain 22-3
    promoted Rear-Admiral 93-4
    pursuit of Villeneuve 198-208
    relations with officers and crew 3, 7,
        27-8, 36, 58, 97, 100, 115-17,
        119-20, 162, 191, 197, 204-5, 211,
        212-13, 216, 221, 221-2, 222-3
    religion 4-5, 219
    strategy and tactics 20-1, 21, 30, 74,
        90-1, 93, 108, 113, 115-17, 160,
        173-4, 190-1, 192-3, 212-14, 218,
        220, 221-3

views on military matters 8, 25, 80-2,
    84, 130-1, 143, 174
will 194, 219
wounds 4, 70, 100, 102-3, 119, 128,
    174
Nelson, Maurice (brother) 178
Nelson, Rev William (brother) 35-6, 48,
    178
Netherlands 36-7, 43, 105-6, 183
Nevis 40, 43, 45-6
New York 29
Nicaragua 24-7, 33
Nile, battle of the 2, 7, 28, 116-24, 146,
    165, 172, 179, 196-7, 210, 214
Nisbet, Dr 46
Nisbet, Josiah 46, 100, 102-3, 104, 153
Nootka Sound crisis 49
Nore mutiny 93, 97
Northwich, Lord 141

Oneglia 83
Orde, Admiral Sir John 9, 114, 196-7, 200,
    208
Orient (Fr) 118-19
Orion, HMS 107, 111-12, 119
Otranto 184
Otway, Captain 164

Paget, Sir A 147
Palermo 131, 133, 135, 137-9, 144-7, 149,
    151, 199
Paoli, Paolo 65
Parker, Admiral Sir Hyde 81, 114, 158-61,
    163-4, 164-8
Parker, Admiral Sir Peter 22
    Lady Parker 22, 35-6, 128
Parker, Captain 104, 174-6
Parker, V/A William 105
Paul I, Czar 5, 124, 158, 166
Peninsula War 28, 52, 99, 192
Piedmont 8, 62, 78-9, 83, 105, 144, 185
Pitt, William, the Younger 44, 49-50, 55,
    58, 106, 121, 158
Porto Ferrajo 86
Portugal 94-5, 111, 128, 137-8, 144, 201
Prince George, HMS 92, 105
Princess Royal, HMS 76
privateers 15, 53-4, 56, 58, 65, 85, 184,
    193
prizes 24-5, 30, 58, 86, 91-2, 95, 97-8,
    122-3, 165, 197, 206

Prussia 43-4, 71, 171

Quebec 15, 29, 45, 81, 168
Queen Charlotte, HMS 146
Queensberry, Duke of 182, 194

Redoutable (Fr) 224-5
Reval 159-60, 166-7
Riou, Captain Edward 163-4
Rochefort, blockade of 205-6
Rodney, Admiral 19, 21, 32, 90, 115
Rome and Papal States 84-5, 129-30, 132,
    144, 185
    blockade of 185
Rosily, Admiral 218-19
Royal Navy
    conventional strategy and tactics 20-1,
        56, 71
    state of 55, 90, 106, 163, 186, 188-9,
        190, 192-3, 195
Royal Sovereign, HMS 223
Ruffo, Cardinal 136, 139-40
Russell, HMS 162
Russia 5, 124, 132, 134, 157-60, 166, 168,
    171, 184

Sabina (Sp) 86
Saints, battle of the 19-20, 21, 29, 32, 55,
    214
Salamanca, battle of 28
San Fiorenzo 64-7, 76-7, 87
San Josef, HMS 158
San Josef (Sp) 91-2, 109, 172
San Juan 26, 29, 123
San Nicolas (Sp) 91-2, 109, 172
San Sebastian 52
Santa Cruz 97-101, 161, 210
Santa Lucia 202
Santissima Trinidad (Sp) 92
Saratoga 16
Sardinia 60, 77, 82, 108, 184-5, 195, 198-9
Saumarez, Captain James 178
Sea Fencibles 174
Seahorse, HMS 14, 100, 140
Seven Years' War 16-19, 115
Shirley, General 39
Sicily 111-14, 127, 131, 133-5, 137, 137-9,
    142, 144-7, 149, 151, 172, 183-4,
    191-2, 198-9
    see also Palermo, Syracuse
Smith, Captain Sir Sydney 9, 134-5

Southey, Robert 36, 141
Spain 49
  as ally of England 58, 62-3, 65, 71
  as ally of France 51-2, 84-101, 105, 107,
    111, 142, 183-4, 191, 196-201, 204
  at Trafalgar 53, 206, 210, 215-18, 224
  in American War of Independence 24,
    31
  makes peace with France 78, 80, 84-5
Spencer, Lord 103, 109, 112, 147, 158
Spithead mutiny 93, 97
St George, HMS 158, 167
St George, Mrs 152, 154
St Kitts 38-40
St Vincent, Admiral Lord, *see* Jervis
St Vincent, battle of *see* Cape St Vincent
Stewart, Colonel 163
Stuart, General Charles 68
Stuart, Don Jacobo 86
Suckling, Captain Maurice (uncle) 12-13,
  14, 22
Suckling, Captain William (uncle) 34-5,
  46
Suffren, Admiral 28
Superb, HMS 201
Suvaroff, General 124, 137, 144, 157
Sweden 157-9, 161, 167
Swiftsure, HMS 118
Switzerland 106
Sykes, John 96
Syracuse 124, 129, 147, 194
Syria 114, 123, 134, 144
  blockade of 123, 126, 144

Téméraire, HMS 223
Tenerife 97-101
Theseus, HMS 97, 100
Thompson, V/A 97
Tippoo Sahib 122
Toulon 20, 58, 62-4, 68-71, 73, 76, 87, 95,
  99, 106, 109, 120, 129, 138, 142,
  146, 182, 186, 188, 196-9
  blockade of 58, 68, 70, 81, 85
  British occupation of 55, 59-61, 71, 88,
    106, 134
  Napoleon captures 62-4J
Trafalgar, battle of 2, 6-7, 55, 120, 195,
  202, 205, 210, 219-25
Trebbia, battle of 144

Trieste 151-2
Trinidad 202
Triumph, HMS 13
Troubridge, Admiral Sir Thomas 89-90,
  98-9, 101, 111-12, 117-18, 123, 128,
  130, 134-7, 141-2, 144, 159, 167,
  175, 178
Tunis 61-2, 88
Turkey 129-31, 134-5, 183-4, 192
Turk's Island 30, 33
Tuscany 71, 79, 81, 84, 181, 185

Unité, HMS 173
USA 37-41
  blockade of 15, 29
  War of Independence 15-16, 21, 29-32,
    34, 55, 105, 115, 158
Ushant, battle of 20

Vado Bay 77
Vanguard, HMS 104, 106-8, 111, 115, 118,
  124, 127-8, 131, 135
Vaudreuil, Admiral 30
Vengeur (Fr) 72
Venice 105
Victory, HMS 181-3, 211, 217, 220, 223-5
Vigo Bay 206
Villeneuve, Admiral 55-6, 198-200, 202,
  205-8, 210-11, 216-20, 223, 225
Voltaire, J-A de 10

Waterloo, battle of 213
Wellington, Arthur Duke of 2, 7-9, 28,
  51-2, 192
West Indies 13, 15, 21, 24-7, 29, 31,
  35-44, 48, 53, 107, 183, 188-9,
  198-9, 201, 203, 206, 208
  see also Barbados, Cuba, Jamaica,
    Leeward Islands, Martinique, Santa
    Lucia
William Henry, Prince, Duke of Clarence
  21, 30, 32, 42-3, 46, 48-9, 103
Winthuysen, Admiral 92
Worcester, HMS 14

Yarmouth 158, 170
Yorktown 31

Zealous, HMS 115, 123